Online Teaching

Vignesh Sundaram

HAWK PRESS

Published by

Hawk Press
4836/24, Ansari Road, Daryaganj
New Delhi – 110 002
Phones : 9643330713, 91-11-23278618, 91-11-35676207
E-mail: thehawkpress@gmail.com
www.thehawkpress.com

ISBN: 978-93-92322-43-3

Contents

Preface

Online teaching is the process of educating others via the internet. Various methods can be used, such as one-on-one video calls, group video calls, and webinars.

You can start teaching from any location (home, coffee shop, co-working space) and enroll students from various backgrounds and geographical areas. Virtually any topic or skill can be taught online.

To teach online, you need to be reasonably comfortable with computers and the internet. This is because interactions with students will take place through messaging platforms, email, and video calls.

The best thing about teaching online is that it's accessible to so many people. Anyone with an internet connection can attend livestream college lectures, learn a language via video-call, or coach themselves through an online video course. Plus, students can participate in interactive discussions through the creation of small groups to examine topics from various perspectives.

E-learning—technology-based education—will change how we count things in higher education. It will bring about a need for new kinds of data to support both policy analyses and management and administrative functions. New analytical conventions will be needed to gain insights about instructional costs, faculty work, and student participation. And new approaches for collecting data, from both learners and learning providers, will need to be developed.

Educational technology is most simply and comfortably defined as an array of tools that might prove helpful in advancing student learning. Educational Technology relies on a broad definition of the word "technology". Technology can refer to material objects of use to humanity, such as machines or hardware, but it can also encompass broader themes, including systems, methods of organization, and techniques. Some modern tools include but are not limited to overhead projectors, laptop computers, and calculators. Newer tools such as "smartphones" and games (both online and offline) are beginning to draw serious attention for their learning potential.

A wide variety of models of e learning have been proposed, which concentrate on different aspects of the development life cycle, and there is a substantial literature on the subject. However the vast majority of this work starts from the point at which the course has already been decided and concentrates on the development and delivery of the course. By contrast there is very little about determining what courses should be selected in relation to institutional strategic plans, and there is little to help course developers determine which parts of the course are best supported by e learning and which by other forms of learning.

Studying along with working has become quite a common trend among the young generation these days. Unlike the past education system, where pupil are required to visit their respective colleges and universities and attend the classes, the modern generation depends on online education. We are grateful to the technological advancements that we are able to reap a long list of benefits in this epoch. Keeping pace with the fast and competitive world, students cannot afford to send two or three years concentrating only on studies.

This book is a steer for those desiring more in depth study of how to integrate a variety of Internet technology tools for successful online learning.

—*Editor*

1

Current Online Teaching Situation

ONLINE EXPERIENCE

A survey was conducted in response to the proliferation of college instructors using the Web as a resource in their teaching. Instead of randomly surveying college instructors about their Web-based teaching needs, experiences, and support mechanisms, this study targeted those with some experience in using the Web as a teaching and learning resource.

The objective of this research was to learn about the common obstacles, supports, and experiences as well as the tools used among early adopters of the Web as a teaching resource.

While the vast majority of our survey respondents had been active in posting course resources, syllabi, or personal information on the Web, not all had previous experience in Web-based instruction. Nearly a quarter of the respondents had never taught even a portion of a course online. On the other hand, nearly 4 in 10 respondents had taught courses partially online; among this group, the average number of partially online courses taught was about four. Another 18 per cent had experience teaching fully online courses, with an average of five such courses. In addition, 19 per cent had done both—partial and completely online courses—with an average of 10 such online course experiences.

Calculations across these responses indicated that nearly 4 in 10 early Web adopters had taught completely online courses, while nearly 6 in 10 had taught at least part of a course online. Given these data, the respondents in this study certainly had extensive online teaching experiences on which to base their survey answers.

Respondent's Web-Related Skills

An instructor's degree of comfort in using different Web technologies has a direct bearing on classroom practices as well as the decision to teach even part of a course online. When instructors are hesitant or lacking in confidence, there is less likelihood for innovation and risk taking.

Therefore, we asked these early Web adopters about their degree of comfort with the following Web skills:

- Creating HTML pages,
- Hosting an online chat,
- Sending and receiving file attachments,
- Using Web-based courseware systems, and
- Moderating a Web-based asynchronous discussion.

The responses were interesting. For instance, over 90 per cent of these faculty members felt a high degree of comfort sending and receiving file attachments in e-mail. Fewer than one per cent of respondents were uncomfortable with this skill. Somewhat surprisingly, 62 per cent were highly comfortable with creating HTML pages and another 20 per cent had a medium level of comfort.

However, this acknowledged degree of comfort likely includes a range of skills from using standard software options such as "save as HTML" to actually being facile with HTML and other programming code. The degree of expertise with HTML remains a question for future surveys. These early adopting faculty were somewhat less comfortable moderating a Web-based asynchronous discussion forum or bulletin board.

Still, nearly 50 per cent rated their degree of comfort as high, while another quarter of them reported a medium level of comfort.

Similarly, 44 per cent were highly comfortable with Web-based courseware systems and another 34 per cent felt moderately comfortable.

On the low end was comfort with hosting an online chat session. Perceptions of online chat tools were roughly split across low, medium, and high comfort categories. These results indicate that these faculty members possessed at least some basic technology skills.

Perhaps, as the NEA survey of traditional and distance learning higher education members revealed, workshops and training sessions on teaching via distance learning are now readily available. While such a skill base and comfort level may be expected of these early Web adopters, many of these faculty members are either taking advantage of university training and support or are engaged in a heavy amount of self-teaching in regard to Web-based teaching tools.

Or perhaps they are overstating their skills. In fact, latter parts of this report reveal a somewhat different picture.

Time Commitments

In terms of overall time investment, these college instructors almost unilaterally agreed that teaching online is more time-consuming than traditional classroom-based instruction. More than 4 in 5 faculty agreed that teaching online courses requires more time than traditional courses.

Fewer than 10 per cent disagreed with that statement. Once again, this is consistent with the NEA report finding that more than half of college faculty teaching via distance learning spent more time on their online courses than their traditional ones regardless of the number of students or times they had previously taught the course. Such findings point to a need for greater course support and incentives that could ease time pressures felt by instructors involved in online teaching.

Attrition

Some reports and media releases contend that students are more likely to drop online courses than traditional ones. Those utilizing a mixed mode or blended approach—traditional and online in the same course – were less likely to experience significant student attrition than those teaching completely online courses.

In fact, only 29 per cent of those utilizing a blended approach experienced more than 10 per cent drop the their courses, whereas 44 per cent of those teaching completely online courses had more than 10 per cent drop their course. Perhaps more strikingly, only 2 per cent of blended courses experienced more than a 50 per cent attrition rate compared to 10 per cent of the completely online courses with such huge attrition rates.

Internet Access

Computer access does not appear to be a problem for these early adopters of Web technologies. Seventy-eight per cent of these college instructors had Internet access in their current or most recent classroom. Computer lab accessibility was even higher with 93 per cent indicating that they had access to an Internet-connected computer lab for class use. Even more, 97 per cent, had Web access from home.

This is more than double the 47 per cent of Americans who are users of the Internet at home as reported in a recent UCLA study. Such high level of technology access is not too surprising given that the majority of the respondents were early Web adopters who had a high level of education.2 In effect, these findings indicate that access to computers and Internet resources is no longer an obstacle for many college faculty.

Platform Choices and Preferences

The delivery platform for online courses is a significant factor in faculty online teaching experiences. Eighty-three per cent of the respondents to this survey indicated that their institution provided a Web-based platform or courseware system for developing online courses or enhancing on-campus courses with online features. Our survey data also indicated that many institutions are utilizing more than one courseware package. In fact, 22 per cent of the respondents worked at institutions that provided access to more than one Web courseware or conferencing platform; when excluding those having yet to adopt a Web courseware system, this increases to 27 per cent. Moreover, 10 per cent provided access to three courseware systems or conferencing tools, and 5 per cent had four or more systems or tools available. When asked what is missing from the courseware tools that they use, slightly over half of the respondents at institutions supporting at least one courseware platform offered some ideas.

The specific features mentioned in their open-ended responses included:

- Ability to annotate documents and visuals in real-time,
- Better grade reporting systems,
- Collaborative white boards,
- Collaborative working tools,
- Drawing software,
- Easy ways to create animations,
- Effective drop box tools,
- Efficient ways to display mathematical notation,
- Electronic library resources,
- Good real-time chat tools,
- Improved quizzes,
- Options for chatting and using PowerPoint at the same time,
- Private asynchronous rooms for group work,
- Proctored testing,

Streaming video,

- Three-dimensional concept visualization tools,
- Tools for tracking student statistics, and,
- 24/7 support.

Of course, many of the tools already exist in the common courseware platforms used in higher education. Other features, such as "options for chatting and using PowerPoint at the same time" are available in various synchronous presentation and collaboration tools often found in corporate training settings. Some general design features requested by these respondents included simplicity, ease of use, user friendliness, enhanced speed, less ugly designs, less cumbersome interfaces, customizability, integration across areas of campus, and flexibility to organize content.

In general, there appeared to be a call for more professional appearance, easy to use features, and functional or usable tools. When asked what they liked about their present courseware tools or system, 56 per cent of the respondents offered ideas.

Instructors preferred:

- Ability to link in lectures with PowerPoint presentations,
- Assignment parts for students to pick up homework,
- Chatrooms,
- Comprehensive tools,
- Consistent course appearance,
- Customizability,
- Data and course security,
- Detailed statistics on bulletin board use,
- Ease of use,
- Flexibility,
- Good online help,
- Internal e-mail systems.
- Online discussion boards,
- Password access,
- Posting of assignments on the Web,
- Posting of deadlines and due dates,
- Randomized test banks,
- Reliability,
- Student drop boxes, and,
- Versatility in quiz types.

QUALITY ONLINE TEACHING

The most important factor affecting student learning is the teacher. Everyone understands, on a personal level, the importance of teachers to their educational success. Teachers who know their subject, understand how to teach and can adjust their teaching to student needs will be successful in raising student achievement, research shows. Teacher expectations also are a significant factor in how much and how well students learn. Online learning provides the opportunity for every middle grades and high school student, regardless of where he or she lives or attends school, to have access to a quality teacher.

Many of these students benefit by being challenged academically by an online teacher who, in some cases, possesses stronger academic credentials and essential teaching skills than traditional classroom staff, especially in certain geographic and subjectshortage areas. Access to quality online teaching can result in improved student academic performance and increased course completion rates. Quality online teaching reflects the attributes of any effective teaching, whether in the traditional classroom or online.

Both traditional classroom teachers and online teachers need to know their subjects and how to teach them. They also must know their students, stay up to date in their subject areas, and manage and monitor students' academic progress to ensure success. But in the 10 years since Web-based courses were first made available to students, the understanding of what is required to be a successful online teacher has increased significantly. The technology used to access and provide Web-based courses effectively also has improved. Now it is important to re-examine what qualifications are needed to be an effective online teacher. Equally important is an understanding of the attributes of today's students, who have access to and can use technology to pursue opportunities and information never before available to them. For many students, this access has changed the way they see the world and the way they work and play.

Consideration of these student issues is critical for a teacher to be effective. Another often overlooked but important issue for online teachers: Delivery of Web-based courses is not restricted to a specific time or schedule. Because instruction does not start and stop at the same time for all students, time-management skills are extremely important, not only for the online teacher but also for students. The lack of these skills is a major reason why some students drop their online courses. Effective online teachers also must possess the ability to prepare quality written communications.

Appropriate and effective writing not only conveys information—it encourages and supports students. Words and body language that traditional classroom teachers use must be translated to the online environment for online teachers to be successful. All of these issues must be factored into setting appropriate standards for quality online teaching.

The Standards

The standards for quality online teaching in this report were developed by knowledgeable, experienced resource persons from K-12 and postsecondary education, drawn from national and regional organizations, SREB state departments of education, and colleges and universities. Through extensive collaboration and sharing with SREB staff over many months, their work culminated in specific standards that SREB states can use to define and implement quality online teaching. Through broad acceptance of these standards, SREB states will be able to provide more students with the courses they need, regardless of where students and teachers reside. These standards have been supported by practice over time, as well as substantiated by research. In fact, research at both the K-12 and postsecondary levels is creating a growing body of evidence that quality online teaching is not only as good as traditional teaching—in many ways it can be superior.

Academic Preparation

- *Standard*: The teacher meets the professional teaching standards established by a state licensing agency or the teacher has academic credentials in the field in which he or she is teaching.
- *Indicators*:
  - *The teacher*:
    a. Meets the state's professional teaching standards or has academic credentials in the field in which he or she is teaching;
    b. Provides evidence that he or she has credentials in the field of study to be taught;
    c. Knows the content of the subject to be taught and understands how to teach the content to students;

d. Facilitates the construction of knowledge through an understanding of how students learn in specific subject areas; and
e. Continues to update academic knowledge and skills.

Content Knowledge, Skills and Temperament for Instructional Technology

- *Standard*: The teacher has the prerequisite technology skills to teach online.
- Indicators
  - *The teacher*:
    a. Demonstrates the ability to effectively use word-processing, spreadsheet and present-ation software;
    b. Demonstrates effective use of Internet browsers, e-mail applications and appropriate online etiquette;
    c. Demonstrates the ability to modify and add content and assessment, using an online Learning Management System;
    d. Incorporates multimedia and visual resources into an online module;
    e. Utilizes synchronous and asynchronous tools effectively;
    f. Troubleshoots typical software and hardware problems;
    g. Demonstrates the ability to effectively use and incorporate subject-specific and develo-pmentally appropriate software in an online learning module; and
    h. Demonstrates growth in technology knowledge and skills in order to stay current with emerging technologies.

Knowledge, Skills and Delivery

- *Standard*: The teacher plans, designs and incor-porates

strategies to encourage active learning, interaction, participation and collaboration in the online environment.

- *Indicators*:
  - *The teacher*:
    a. Demonstrates effective strategies and techniques that actively engage students in the learning process;
    b. Facilitates and monitors appropriate interaction among students;
    c. Builds and maintains a community of learners by creating a relationship of trust, demonstrating effective facilitation skills, establishing consistent and reliable expectations, and supporting and encouraging independence and creativity;
    e. Promotes learning through group inter-action;
    f. Leads online instruction groups that are goal-oriented, focused, project-based and inquiry-oriented;
    g. Demonstrates knowledge and responds appropriately to the cultural background and learning needs of non-native English speakers;
    h. Differentiates instruction based on students' learning styles and needs and assists students in assimilating information to gain understanding and knowledge; and
    i. Demonstrates growth in teaching strategies in order to benefit from current research and practice.
- *Standard*: The teacher provides online leadership in a manner that promotes student success through regular feedback, prompt response and clear expectations.
- *Indicators*:
  - *The teacher:*
    a. Consistently models effective communi-cation skills and maintains records of applicable communications with students;

b. Encourages interaction and cooperation among students, encourages active learning, provides prompt feedback, communicates high expectations, and respects diverse talents and learning styles;
c. Persists, in a consistent and reasonable manner, until students are successful; z establishes and maintains ongoing and frequent teacher-student interaction, student-student interaction and teacher-parent interaction;
d. Provides an online syllabus that details the terms of class interaction for both teacher and students, defines clear expectations for both teacher and students, defines the grading criteria, establishes inappropriate bahaviour criteria for both teacher and students, and explains the course organiz-ation to students;
e. Provides a syllabus with objectives, concepts and learning outcomes in a clearly written, concise format;
f. Uses student data to inform instruction, guides and monitors students' management of their time, monitors learner progress with available tools and develops an intervention plan for unsuccessful learners;
g. Provides timely, constructive feedback to students about assignments and questions;
h. Gives students clear expectations about teacher response time.

- *Standard*: The teacher models, guides and encourages legal, ethical, safe and healthy bahaviour related to technology use.
- *Indicators*:
  - *The teacher*:

a. Facilitates student investigations of the legal and ethical issues related to technology and society;

b. Establishes standards for student bahaviour that are designed to ensure academic integrity and appropriate uses of the Internet and written communication;
c. identifies the risks of academic dishonesty for students;
d. Demonstrates an awareness of how the use of technology may impact student testing performance;
f. Uses course content that complies with intellectual property rights policies and fair use standards;
g. Provides students with an understanding of the importance of Acceptable Use Policies;
h. Demonstrates knowledge of resources and techniques for dealing with issues arising from inappropriate use of electronically accessed data or information; and
i. Informs students of their right to privacy and the conditions under which their names or online submissions may be shared with others.

- *Standard*: The teacher has experienced online learning from the perspective of a student.
- *Indicators*:
  - *The teacher*:
    a. Applies experiences as an online student to develop and implement successful strategies for online teaching;
    b. Demonstrates the ability to anticipate challenges and problems in the online classroom; and
    c. Demonstrates an understanding of the perspective of the online student through appropriate responsiveness and a supportive attitude towards students.
- *Standard*: The teacher understands and is responsive to students with special needs in the online classroom.

- *Indicators:*
  - *The teacher:*
    a. Understands that students have varied talents and skills and uses appropriate strategies designed to include all students;
    b. Provides activities, modified as necessary, that are relevant to the needs of all students;
    c. Adapts and adjusts instruction to create multiple paths to learning objectives;
    d. Encourages collaboration and interaction among all students;
    e. Exhibits the ability to assess student knowledge and instruction in a variety of ways; and
    f. Provides student-centered sessions and activities that are based on concepts of active learning and that are connected to real-world applications.
- *Standard*: The teacher demonstrates competencies in creating and implementing assessments in online learning environments in ways that assure validity and reliability of instruments and procedures.
- *Indicators*:
  - *The teacher:*
    a. Creates or selects fair, adequate and appropriate assessment instruments to measure online learning that reflect sufficient content validity, reliability and consistency over time; and
    b. Implements online assessment measures and materials in ways that ensure instrument validity and reliability.
- *Standard*: The teacher develops and delivers assessments, projects and assignments that meet standards-based learning goals and assesses learning progress by measuring student achievement of learning goals.
- *Indicators*:
  - *The teacher:*

a. Continually reviews all materials and Web resources for their alignment with course objectives and state and local standards and for their appropriateness;
b. Creates assignments, projects and assessments that are aligned with students' different visual, auditory and hands-on ways of learning;
c. Includes authentic assessment as part of the evaluation process;
d. Provides continuous evaluation of students to include pre- and post-testing and student input throughout the course; and
e. Demonstrates an understanding of the relationships between and among the assignments, assessments and standards-based learning goals.

- *Standard*: The teacher demonstrates competencies in using data and findings from assessments and other data sources to modify instructional methods and content and to guide student learning.
- *Indicators*:
  - *The teacher*:
    a. Assesses each student's background and content knowledge and uses these data to plan instruction;
    b. Reviews student responses to test items to identify issues related to test validity or instructional effectiveness;
    c. Uses observational data to monitor course progress and effectiveness; and
    d. Creates opportunities for self-reflection or assessment of teaching effectiveness within the online environment.
- *Standard*: The teacher demonstrates frequent and effective strategies that enable both teacher and students to complete self- and pre-assessments.
- *Indicators:*
  - *The teacher*:
    a. Employs ways to assess student readiness for course content and method of delivery;

b. Employs ways for students to effectively evaluate and assess their own readiness for course content and method of delivery;
c. Understands that student success is an important measure of teaching and course success; and
d. Provides opportunities for student self-assessment within courses.

COMPETENCIES FOR ONLINE TEACHING

Information technology is changing the way people live and learn. Not surprisingly information technology is also transformation the nature of teaching. These remarks provide a framework for thinking about such changes and exploring work in progress that is relevant to the development of competencies specific to teaching online.

Competence, Competencies and Certification

Competence refers to a state of being well qualified to perform an activity, task or job function. When a person is competent to do something, he or she has achieved a state of competence that is recognizable and verifiable to a particular community of practitioners.

A competency, then, refers to the way that a state of competence can be demonstrated to the relevant community. According to the International Board of Standards for Training, Performance and Instruction, a competency involves a related set of knowledge, skills and attitudes that enable a person to effectively perform the activities of a given occupation or function in such a way that meets or exceeds the standards expected in a particular profession or work setting.

The structure and assessment of competencies may differ from one community of practice to another and even within a community. To facilitate a common understanding of competencies in the context of online and distributed learning some specifications have been elaborated. Typically, a competency is divided into specific indicators describing the requisite knowledge, skills, attitudes and context of performance. There are different ways to validate that a person has demonstrated the relevant competencies. One of them is through a certification process. Teacher certification is a common practice, and the notion of teacher competencies is fairly well established.

However, competencies are generally associated with highly formalized professional activities and not applied to ill-defined tasks. Ill-defined tasks certainly include many forms of teaching. This narrow view of competence runs counter to common sense and professional practice, but brings into attention the mainstream approach to elaboration of teacher competencies where it is essential to clearly identify the conditions of teaching. The delivery environment is a particularly relevant condition to identify competencies for online teaching.

Online and Classroom Teaching

Information technology can be integrated into both online and classroom settings, but the interaction between these technologies and new approaches to learning and instruction may vary. The range of activities available in online settings and the multiple conditions of time in which they take place are evidence that the technology demands placed on online teachers are somewhat more significant than those associated with classroom teachers. Much of what has already been published with regard to online teaching has focused on technical skills and requirements of successfully moderating and facilitating online discussions and chat sessions. This body of literature suggests that becoming an effective online moderator requires training and that there are competencies unique to online environments. In online asynchronous discussions, the moderator's competencies involve allowing learners time for reflection, keeping discussions alive and on a productive path, and archiving and organizing discussions to be used in subsequent sessions.

In online synchronous discussions, the moderator must establish ground rules for discussion, animate interactions with minimal instructor intervention, sense how online text messages may appear to distant learners, and be aware of cultural differences. How are these competencies unique to online teaching? At the applied level, animating discussions, displaying cultural sensitivity and so on, apply to all teachers. At the environment level, however, the ways in which a teacher demonstrates such competence is quite different, which suggests that there are competencies unique to online settings. According to Belisle and Linard the use of IT in teaching calls for additional competencies adapted to new roles and circumstances. Teaching competencies and online teaching competencies have generally been considered separately. However, efforts to interrelate the two are being undertaken by IBSTPI in association with the research centre for Téluq-université, Université de Québec.

Implications of Competencies for Online Teaching

The current interest in competencies for online teaching is coming from business and industry, primarily with regard to technical training and professional development courses offered in online settings.

It is quite likely that some of the interest in competencies for online teaching is a result of hastily-crafted online courses and inadequate preparation of online facilitators. Clearly technology offers the potential to create and implement highly engaging and effective online environments to support a wide variety of learning goals. It is also quite clear that our capacity to make effective use of information technology in educational settings is impaired by inadequate preparation of teachers and by a shortage of properly trained instructional designers and educational support personnel.

The development of competencies for online teaching should lead to the associated development of training for online teachers and to the certification of online teachers. To develop competencies for online teachers is not without challenge. Competencies are dynamic in nature, and they largely depend on the relevant social context. The constant transformation of IT makes the development of competencies for online teachers a continuous process and demands continuing professional preparation and training for online teachers. Such endeavors will improve our ability to make effective use of technology in learning and instruction.

PREPARING TO TEACH ONLINE

As you plan your online course, it is helpful to remember that in any environment "good teaching is good teaching". Experienced online instructors stress that teaching online is less about the mechanics of distance education and "more about what makes for an effective educational experience, regardless of where or when it is delivered". Many teachers have found the Principles of Good Practice in Undergraduate Education to be a useful framework for thinking about how to enhance student learning in their classes.

Principles of Good Practice in Undergraduate Education:

- Encourages contact between students and faculty, especially contact focused on the academic agenda.
- Develops reciprocity and cooperation among students, *i.e.*, teaching students to work productively with others.
- Encourages active learning, *i.e.*, doing and thinking about the learning process.
- Gives prompt feedback and helps students understand how to respond.
- Emphasizes time on task by providing repeated useful, productive, guided practice.
- Communicates high expectations and encourages students to have high self-expectations.
- Respects diverse talents and ways of learning and engenders respect of intellectual diversity.

An additional good practice that does not appear on this list, but that many experienced online instructors mention as being essential to successful teaching, is:

- Includes a well-organized course, the structure of which is clearly communicated to students.

Use these eight best practices as a framework for thinking about your online course.

Of course, it is also important to acknowledge that some aspects of good teaching, such as faculty-student contact and cooperation among students, are particularly challenging to accomplish in an online environment. This recommendations on how to accomplish these goals, despite the complications that may exist.

Preparing Students to Learn Online

Students new to online learning may initially find this kind of learning disorienting without the physical classroom space and guidance from the physical presence of a teacher. Other students may initially misperceive learning online as "easier" than learning in a physical classroom space. In reality, students often find the workload in an online course heavier because they must cover course material on their own and type their discussion comments.

There are a number of suggestions for how to help prepare students for online learning:

- *Clarify computer skills/terminology*:
  - Provide guidelines that detail the minimum technological requirements needed for the course.
  - At the beginning of the semester, provide a detailed worksheet with instructions on how to complete the technical tasks required for completing course work. For example, while it may be clear to you how to post a message for many students, such tasks are new. Also, while some students may be familiar with one online environment, do not assume that they are familiar with all online environments. Some examples of information to provide include:

    Where to find information online

    How to post a message and homework assign-ments

    How to access course readings and take online exams
  - Describe how to seek help immediately when having trouble
  - Explain online conventions for tone, such as using ALL CAPS for emphasis. Set rules for using abbreviations and emoticons.
  - Provide a tutorial on computer basics.
    a. *Tip*: If you cannot provide a tutorial on computer basics, try working with a local community college to schedule a series of computer orientations. One Online Fellow scheduled five 2-hour computer orientations at a local community college to help

her students learn computer basics. The college's IT staff setup 15 computers with updated browsers and word processing. Students learned basic computer operation as well as word processing skills. The final tutorial was dedicated to navigating library databases and the World Wide Web. The collaborative effort helped ensure student success for those students unfamiliar with online learning.

- *Explain the differences in learning online versus learning in a traditional classroom*:
  - Emphasize the amount of time needed for taking an online class and the importance of working independently. Because all class discussions are written, students must be prepared for the amount of time needed to type their comments. A 3-credit online course can easily require more than six hours of time, especially for students who type slowly.
  - Emphasize the extensiveness of reading and writing in an online course. Because all class assignments are provided in written format with no opportunity for class questions, teachers detail class assignments thoroughly in online courses. Consequently, students must become careful readers in order to ensure that they understand the assignment.
  - To help students understand the communication differences of learning online, provide a detailed worksheet with instructions on communication guidelines.
    a. *Tip*: Conventions for Communicating Online to this stage for an example.
    b. *Tip*: One instructor uses the following explanation to clarify to her students the definition of a threaded discussion post:

       How much to post, and what makes a "good" post?: These are hard questions to answer because discussions are organic, developing and evolving depending upon what is said by whom. In general, posting only once is not enough to really engage in a discussion. I am expecting probably 3-6 posts depending upon the amount of time I've allotted for the discussion and how in-depth your posts are. What I expect and hope to see is a dialogue evolving, with give and take, back and forth, questions asked and ideas explored like in a face-to-face class discussion. So as you post be cognizant that you are engaging in a discussion. Do not post long pages of responses—probably a couple of paragraphs at most, sometimes a sentence or two can be effective, especially if you're asking a question.

- *Address students' concerns on cyber-culture anxiety*:
  - Encourage questions and comments about technology.
  - Use a survey to assess student technical knowledge at the beginning of the semester.
    a. *Tip*: The Pre/Post Survey example in this stage for ways to assess student technical knowledge.
- *Clarify expectations*:
  - Post guidelines for participation on the class homepage. For example, explain to students how many days each week they should login to the course website. In online courses, it is not uncommon to expect students to login every week day.
  - Give a detailed, conspicuous course outline. Because you must clarify course expectations only in writing, make sure that you give students enough detail to complete class assignments. Even simple assignments like a journal need detailed explanations.
    a. *Tip*: One instructor uses the following explanation for the weekly journal exercise. She posts this explanation in every unit to remind students weekly of the assignment:

       Your journal is the place for you to keep thinking about, wrestling with, exploring the issues we've discussed online. Feel free to add your own day-to-day observations about issues related to our course. Your journal is only read by me. I will never comment on your observations; I only check to If you've completed the assignment. Length: 1-2 paragraphs Due: Every Friday by midnight EST

- Set clear expectations with regard to student performance/activity. Help students understand expectations for the course and encourage them to ask questions. One way to help students understand course expectations is to post examples of model assignments. You can post examples of model assignments from other webpages or upload sample papers. Most online course software programmes allow you to easily upload files, such as MS Word and Excel documents.
- Remind students frequently of course expectations.
    a. *Tip*: During the semester, one instructor posted reminders to keep students up-to-date with the course material. Following is an example of one such reminder: Have you read your James McBride?: If you haven't started reading The Colour of Water, you better get reading!It's almost Monday and the weekly exercise is due Wednesday. Look forthe threaded discussion posting on Monday morning.Hope you had a great weekend! I look forward to getting your responsepapers on Monday night!
- Explain the time-frame in which e-mails will be answered. For example, on Monday, Wednesday, and Friday only, or within 2 business days of receipt.
- Emphasize courtesy to fellow students. Because students can not see verbal or visual clues from other speakers, encourage them to be tactful in their responses or include parenthetical clues for humour or emotion.
    a. *Tip*: One instructor describes courtesy to her students with the following explanation:

Our online discussions will be class discussions, meaning the same respect we would show each other in an actual classroom, as suggested, also show in a virtual classroom.

In fact, because the online environment is primarily a verbal environment where we communicate through writing, it lacks the physical and auditory clues that accompany face-to-face discussion, which may lead to more misunderstandings, particularly when a person is using humour.

FUTURE OF ONLINE TEACHING

Institutions of higher education have increasingly embraced online education, and the number of students enrolled in distance programmes is rapidly rising in colleges and universities throughout the United States. In response to these changes in enrollment demands, many states, institutions, and organizations have been working on strategic plans to implement online education.

At the same time, misconceptions and myths related to the difficulty of teaching and learning online, technologies available to support online instruction, the support and compensation needed for high-quality instructors, and the needs of online students create challenges for such vision statements and planning documents. In part, this confusion swells as higher education explores dozens of e-learning technologies with new ones seeming to emerge each week. Such technologies confront instructors and administrators at a time of continued budget retrenchments and rethinking. Adding to this dilemma, bored students are dropping out of online classes while pleading for richer and more engaging online learning experiences.

Given the demand for online learning, the plethora of online technologies to incorporate into teaching, the budgetary problems, and the opportunities for innovation, we argue that online learning environments are facing a "perfect e-storm," linking pedagogy, technology, and learner needs. Considering the extensive turbulence created by the perfect storm surrounding e-learning, it is not surprising that opinions are mixed about the benefits of online teaching and learning in higher education. As illustrated in numerous issues of the Chronicle of Higher Education during the past decade, excitement and enthusiasm for e-learning alternate with a pervasive sense of e-learning gloom, disappointment, bankruptcy and lawsuits, and myriad other contentions. Appropriately, the question arises as to where online learning is headed.

Navigating online education requires an understanding of the current state and the future direction of online teaching and learning. The study described here surveyed instructors and administrators in postsecondary institutions, mainly in the United States, to explore future trends of online education. In particular, the study makes predictions regarding the changing roles of online instructors, student expectations and needs related to online learning, pedagogical innovation, and projected technology use in online teaching and learning.

We began this project with a review of past studies of the issues and trends in online teaching and learning in higher education.

2

Online Teaching and Learning

A recent survey of higher education in the United States reported that more than 2.35 million students enrolled in online courses in fall 2004. This report also noted that online education is becoming an important long-term strategy for many postsecondary institutions. Given the rapid growth of online education and its importance for postsecondary institutions, it is imperative that institutions of higher education provide quality online programmes.

The literature addresses student achievement and satisfaction as two means to assess the quality of online education. Studies focused on academic achievement have shown mixed reviews, but some researchers point out that online education can be at least as effective as traditional classroom instruction.

Several research studies on student satisfaction in online courses or programmes reported both satisfied and dissatisfied students. Faculty training and support is another critical component of quality online education. Many researchers posit that instructors play a different role from that of traditional classroom instructors when they teach online courses, as well as when they teach residential courses with Web enhancements. Such new roles for online instructors require training and support. Some case studies of faculty development programmes indicate that such programmes can have positive impacts on instructor transitions from teaching in a face-to-face to an online setting.

Pedagogy and Technology for online Education

Several research studies have covered effective pedagogical strategies for online teaching. Partlow and Gibbs, for instance, found from a Delphi study of experts in instructional technology and constructivism that online courses designed from constructivist principles should be relevant, interactive, project- based, and collaborative, while providing learners with some choice or control over their learning. Additionally, Keeton investigated effective online instructional practices based on a framework of effective teaching practices in face-to-face instruction in higher education. In this study, Keeton interviewed faculty in postsecondary institutions, who rated the effectiveness of online instructional strategies. These instructors gave higher ratings to online instructional strategies that "create an environment that supports and encourages inquiry," "broaden the learner's experience of the subject matter," and "elicit active and critical reflection by learners on their growing experience base."

In another study of pedagogical practices, Bonk found that only 23–45 per cent of online instructors surveyed actually used online activities related to critical and creative thinking, handson performances, interactive labs, data analysis, and scientific simulations, although 40 per cent of the participants said those activities were highly important in online learning environments.

In effect, a significant gap separated preferred and actual online instructional practices. Technology has played and continues to play an important role in the development and expansion of online education.

Accordingly, many universities have reported an increase in the use of online tools. Over the past decade, countless efforts have sought to integrate emerging Internet technologies into the teaching and learning process in higher education. Several studies have reported cases related to the use of blogs to promote student collaboration and reflection.

Some researchers also have promoted the plausibility of using wikis for online student collaboration, and podcasting is beginning to garner attention from educators for its instructional use.

Although some discussions in the literature relate to effective practices in the use of emerging technologies for online education, empirical evidence to support or refute the effectiveness of such technologies, or, perhaps more importantly, guidance on how to use such tools effectively based on empirical evidence, is lacking.

Method

This study was based on a survey of individuals believed to have relevant experience with and insights into the factors affecting the present and future state of online education.

Participants

An online survey was conducted of college instructors and administrators who were members of either the Multimedia Educational Resource for Learning and Online Teaching (MERLOT) or the Western Cooperative for Educational Telecommunications (WCET), both premier associations for online education. MERLOT is a free and open resource for higher education with membership that, at the time of this study, included more than 12,000 college professors, instructional designers, and administrators who share and peer-evaluate their Web resources and materials (today, MERLOT has more than 35,000 members).

WCET is an organization with 500-600 members that provides resources and information regarding the effective use of telecommunications technology in learning. Also surveyed were those who had posted one or more course syllabi at the World Lecture Hall (WLH), which has approximately 2,000 members and was developed by the University of Texas for faculty to share syllabi. This study is a part of a longitudinal effort to understand the use of technology in teaching, within both higher education and corporate training settings. The second author had previously surveyed MERLOT and WLH members on the state of online learning as well as corporate trainers on online training and blended learning.

Instrument

Using an online survey service, SurveyShare, we developed

an online questionnaire as an instrument for this survey study. The questionnaire consisted of 42 questions grouped into three parts related to the current status and future trends of online education in higher education. The first part included 10 questions regarding respondents' demographic information. The second part included seven questions about the current status of online learning at the respondents' organizations. The third part included items regarding predictions about online teaching and learning. The survey used various types of questions, including Likert-type, multiple-choice, and open-ended questions.

Data Collection and Analysis

The survey took place from late November 2003 to early January 2004. An invitation was sent by e-mail to the sample of instructors, instructional designers, and administrators described earlier. The e-mail included information about the study as well as the URL to the survey site. Of more than 12,000 who received the e-mail request, 562 completed the survey. The participants responded to the survey anonymously, and the data were stored in the hosted online survey service. Descriptive data analyses (such as frequencies) were conducted using the data analysis tool provided in the online survey site.

Results

Our study confirmed some commonly held beliefs about online education, refuted others, and provided a range of predictions about the future of technology- enabled education.

Demographics of Online Instructors

Sixty-six per cent of the survey respondents held teaching positions (professors, instructors, or lecturers), while nearly one-fourth were administrators or instructional designers. Respondents represented institutions of various types: approximately half were employed by public, four-year colleges or universities; 23 per cent by community colleges or vocational institutes; and 16 per cent by private postsecondary institutions. A large majority (87 per cent) said their institutions offer online courses, and about 70 per cent of them had taught online courses. The experience with online teaching varied from none to more than 10 years.

Although not every respondent had online teaching experience, more than 95 per cent had experience integrating computer or Web technology into their face-to-face teaching. Survey results show that women appear to be teaching online in far greater numbers than just a few years ago. In fact, more than half of the respondents (53 per cent) were women. Such findings were surprising because a similar study conducted a few years earlier was dominated by male instructors who were full professors at tier-one universities. Perhaps female instructors had become more comfortable teaching and sharing activities online during the few years that elapsed between surveys, or perhaps support for instructors had improved on college campuses, or both.

Emerging Technology

When asked about several emerging technologies for online education, 27 per cent of respondents predicted that use of course management systems (CMSs) would increase most drastically in the next five years. Those surveyed also said that video streaming, online testing and exam tools, and learning object libraries would find significantly greater use on campus during this time.

Between 5 and 10 per cent of respondents expected to see increases in asynchronous discussion tools, videoconferencing, synchronous presentation tools, and online testing. The survey also asked what technology would most impact the delivery of online learning during the next five years.

Respondents could select one of 14 key technologies. About 18 per cent of respondents predicted that reusable content objects and wireless technologies would have the most significant impact. Smaller percentages (from 7 to almost 14 per cent) selected peer-to-peer collaboration, digital libraries, simulations and games, assistive technologies, and digital portfolios.

In contrast, less than 5 per cent predicted that e-books, intelligent agents, Tablet PCs, virtual worlds, language support, and wearable technologies would have significant impact on the delivery of online learning.

These findings seem to reflect the perceived importance of online technologies for sharing and using preexisting content.

Additionally, respondents predicted that advances in Internet technology (for example, greatly extended bandwidth and wireless Internet connections) are likely to increase the use of multimedia and interactive simulations or games in online learning during the next five to 10 years.

Only about one in 10, however, predicted that advances in Internet technology would enhance videoconferencing or international collaboration, and just one in 16 thought it might offer greater chances to interact with field experts or practitioners.

Again, the focus was on enhancing content and associated content delivery, not on the social interactions, cross-cultural exchanges, or new feedback channels that wider bandwidth could offer.

Such responses indicate that respondents still see learning as content-driven, not based on social interactions and distributed intelligence. The emphasis remains on a knowledge-transmission approach to education, not one rich in peer feedback, online mentoring, or cognitive apprenticeship.

Enormous Learner Demands

Our study revealed a number of trends related to areas of growth in online education, future needs for online instructors, and the dominance of online versus face-to-face instruction.

Growth of Online Programmes/Degrees

Comparing current online offerings and projected future online offerings at respondents' institutions yields predictions about the areas of growth in online programmes and degrees. Most respondents expected considerable growth in online certification and recertification programmes in the next few years, as well as in associate's degrees. Yet, our survey respondents predicted little growth in the number of institutions that offer online master's or doctoral programmes in the future.

Although more than half of the respondents (54 per cent)

expected that their institutions would offer online master's or doctoral programmes in the coming years, almost the same number of respondents (53 per cent) reported that their institutions were presently offering online master's or doctoral programmes. In contrast, respondents predicted that certification and recertification programmes would see 10-20 per cent growth from present offerings. Such responses indicate that higher education institutions might be wise to explore certificate and shortprogram offerings rather than full degree programmes.

Online Instructors' Readiness

Will online instructors be ready to meet the challenges brought by the projected increases in learner demands for online education? About half of the respondents predicted that monetary support for and pedagogical competency of online instructors would most significantly affect the success of their online programmes. In addition, instructors' technical competency was the third most pressing factor. Nevertheless pedagogical skill was deemed more important than technological skill for effective online teaching. With regard to the needs for pedagogical competency of online instructors, a majority of the respondents expected that online instructors would typically have received some sort of training in online teaching either internally or externally by the year 2010.

The Rise of Blended Learning

The survey asked respondents for their predictions related to the growth of online education in the next few years. Respondents indicated that more emphasis is expected on blended learning-instruction that combines face-to-face with online offerings-than on fully online courses. Those surveyed predicted a distinct shift from about onequarter of classes being blended today to perhaps the vast majority of courses having some Web component by the end of the decade.

Enhanced Pedagogy

Although the use of CMSs in higher education has increased rapidly and is likely the foundation for the rapid increase in the number of online learners during the past decade, some researchers argue that CMSs are promoted as ways to manage learners rather than to promote rich, interactive experiences. As a result, enhancing pedagogy is perhaps the most important factor in navigating the perfect e-storm. In the present study, respondents made predictions about the quality of online education in the near future and about how online courses would be taught and evaluated.

The Quality of Future Online Education

Survey respondents generally agreed with recent Sloan reports that the quality of online education will improve in the future. Sixty per cent of respondents expected that the quality of online courses would be identical to traditional instruction by the year 2006. Also, a majority of the respondents predicted that the quality of online courses would be superior to (47 per cent) or the same as (39 per cent) that of traditional instruction by 2013. Only 8 per cent predicted that the quality of online courses would be inferior in 2013. Similarly, a large majority of respondents predicted that learning outcomes of online students would be either the same as (39 per cent) or superior to (42 per cent) those of traditionally taught students by 2013.

In effect, the trend is for course quality and learner outcomes to steadily and significantly improve during the coming decade. Although we did not ask about reasons for the increase in quality, such numbers should be interesting and valuable to administrators, instructors, students, and other online learning stakeholders.

In terms of factors that can improve online learners' success, respondents said that training students to selfregulatetheir learning (22 per cent) was needed most, followed by better measures of student readiness (17 per cent), better evaluation of student achievement (17 per cent), and better CMSs to track student learning. Nine per cent said additional technology training is needed. This concern about learner self-regulationis ironic in a world dominated and driven by learning management systems that are primarily used to manage students, as alluded to earlier. Follow-up surveys might address whether learners per- ceive this mixed message and whether they prefer to be managed online or engage in more self-directed online environments. As Carmean and Haefner argued, there is a need for CMS environments that foster deeper student learning and engagement. They noted that such environments might foster student choice among various activities, reflection, apprenticeship, synthesis, real-world problem solving, and rich, timely feedback.

More recently, Weigel added to this argument by suggesting that the next-generation CMS should foster a more learner-centered environment that rich in critical thinking, student exploration, peer learning and knowledge construction, interdisciplinary experiences incorporating a community of educators (practitioners, business leaders, alumni, and others), and educational opportunities.

Online Teaching Skills

Instructors' abilities to teach online are critical to the quality of online education. Unlike our earlier study related to the state of online learning in 2001, which included many questions about online learning tools and features, the present study focused more on learning outcomes and pedagogical skills. For instance, this study found that the most important skills for an online instructor during the next few years will be how to moderate or facilitate learning and how to develop or plan for high-quality online courses. Being a subject-matter expert was the next most important skill. In effect, the results indicate that planning and moderating skills are perhaps more important than actual "teaching" or lecturing skills in online courses. As Salmon pointed out, online instructors are moderators or facilitators of student learning.

Pedagogical Techniques

Over half of the survey respondents predicted that online collaboration, casebased learning, and problem-based learning (PBL) would be the preferred instructional methods for online instructors in the coming decade. In contrast, few respondents expected that instructors would rely on lectures, modeling, or Socratic instruction for their online teaching in the future. In other words, survey respondents predicted that more learner-centered techniques would be used in the future, indicating a marked shift from traditional teacher-directed approaches. Existing research indicates that online instructors tend to use easy-toimplement tools, resources, and strategies rather than complex PBL, virtual teaming, cross-cultural collaboration, simulations, and other forms of rich interactive media.

If the prediction for more learner-centered pedagogies online is realised, it would be interesting to study whether those teaching online transfer such pedagogical skills to their face-to-face instructional activities. Our findings also indicated that, in general, respondents envisioned the Web in the next few years more as a tool for virtual teaming or collaboration, critical thinking, and enhanced student engagement than as an opportunity for student idea generation and expression of creativity. This is not surprising, given that most instruction in higher education is focused on consumption and evaluation of knowledge, not on the generation of it. Perhaps online training departments and units need to offer more examples of how to successfully embed creative and generative online tasks and activities.

Evaluation and Assessment of Online Courses

Evaluation is an important part of ensuring the quality of online courses and programmes. When asked how the quality of online education will be most effectively measured during the coming decade, 44 per cent answered that a comparison of online student achievement with that of students in face-to-face classroom settings would be the most effective, followed by student performance in simulated tasks of real-world activities (15 per cent), calculations of return on investment (10 per cent), and student course evaluations (9 per cent). Clearly, respondents believe that face-to-face instruction provides a valid benchmark for teaching and learning outcomes and that online performance should at least equal its effectiveness. Such views, while politically important, seem to forget that much of the learning that occurs online could not take place in a faceto- face delivery mode (for example, asynchronous online discussions or online mentoring). It also assumes that face-to-face instruction is superior. What if institutions took the opposite stance and measured face-to-face courses based on whether they could accomplish all that online instruction can?

As for the forms of evaluation that will be used during the next few years, respondents predicted that online practice quizzes and exams would be most highly used, followed by online surveying and polling, course evaluations, and online quizzes and exams. In particular, more than 90 per cent of the respondents predicted that online surveys would be used as an important student research tool or as a teaching device in addition to student assessment and course evaluation. This finding affirms our belief that online surveys offer the chance to be learner-centered because they allow students to collect, analyse, and report on real-world data and projects.

APPROACHES TO ONLINE LEARNING

Two approaches to online learning have emerged: synchronous and asynchronous learning. Synchronous learning is instruction and collaboration in "real time" via the Internet.

It typically involves tools, such as:

- Live chat
- Audio and video conferencing
- Data and application sharing
- Shared whiteboard
- Virtual "hand raising"
- Joint viewing of multimedia presentations and online slide shows

Asynchronous learning methods use the time-delayed capabilities of the Internet.

It typically involves tools, such as:

- e-mail
- Threaded discussion
- Newsgroups and bulletin boards
- File attachments

Asynchronous courses are still instructor-facilitated but are not conducted in real time, which means that students and teacher can engage in course-related activities at their convenience rather than during specifically coordinated class sessions. In asynchronous courses, learning does not need to be scheduled in the same way as synchronous learning, allowing students and instructors the benefits of anytime, anywhere learning.

Course Software

Rather than creating your online course from scratch, a number of software programmes are now available that make it easy to develop an online course. These programmes include features such as threaded discussions and document sharing and pre-designed design layouts to make the course design process easier. Check with the campus technology specialists to learn more about the preferred software for online learning in your department.

Advantages of Learning Online

Online learning offers a variety of educational opportunities:

- *Student-centered learning*: The variety of online tools draw on individual learning styles and help students become more versatile learners.
- *Collaborative learning*: Online group work allows students to become more active participants in the learning process. Contributing input requires that students comprehend what is being discussed, organize their thinking coherently, and express that thinking with carefully
- *Easy access to global resources*: Students can easily access online databases and subject experts in the online classroom.
- *Experiential learning through multimedia presentations*: New technologies can be used to engage and motivate students. Technology can also be used to support students in their learning activities.
- *Accessible for non-traditional students*: Online delivery of programmes and courses makes participation possible for students who experience geographic and time barriers in gaining access to higher education.
- *Draws on student interest in online learning*: Many students are interested in online learning. In a recent survey

conducted by the Office of Academic Planning and Assessment at UMass Amherst, more than 50% of students surveyed said that they were "very interested" or "somewhat interested" in taking an online course.

Advantages of Teaching Online

Teaching online courses can:

- *Offer the opportunity to think about teaching in new ways*: Online teaching can allow you to experiment with techniques only available in online environments, such as threaded discussions and webliographies.
- *Provide ideas and techniques to implement in traditional courses*: Online e-mail discussions, a frequently-used practice in online learning, can be incorporated into traditional courses to facilitate group work. Other techniques, such as web-based course calendars and sample papers posted on the Internet can easily be incorporated into a traditional course.
- *Expand the reach of the curriculum*: Online teaching can expand existing curriculum to students on a regional, national, and international level.
- *Professional satisfaction*: Teaching online can be an enormously rewarding experience for teachers. Teachers often cite the diversity of students in online courses as one of the most rewarding aspects of teaching online.
- *Instructor convenience*: Teaching online can offer teachers conveniences not available in traditional classroom settings; for example, at-home office hours and flexible work schedules.

Challenges of Teaching Online

According to a recent American Federation of Teachers report on distance learning, faculty must be prepared to meet the special requirements of teaching at a distance.

Some of the challenges for instructors of teaching online include:

- Familiarity with the online environment
- Capacity to use the medium to its advantage

- Being available to students on an extended basis electronically
- Providing quick responses and feedback to students

Yet, the proponents of online learning argue that these obstacles can be overcome by employing such techniques as the following:

- *Become familiar with the technology used in your online course*: Long before your course starts, become familiar with the technology used in your online course, including hardware and software, and spend some time exploring their options. An online course requires a high level of computing power and reliable telecommunications infrastructure. Make sure you have access to both.
- *Use the online medium to your advantage*: The online environment is essentially a space for written communication. This is both a limitation and a potential of online learning. Written communication can be more time consuming, but "the ability to sit and think as one composes a question or comment also can raise the quality of discussion." Additionally, shy students who have trouble participating in a classroom discussion often feel more comfortable in an online classroom. Online classrooms can be developed with this fact in mind to take advantage of these considerations.
- *Keep connected with students*: Use the technology of the online environment to help you keep in touch with students. Communicate frequently with students, both individually and as a group. A main part of this focuses on how to connect with students. While keeping connected with students can be a challenge, the online environment offers a number of interesting pedagogical opportunities.

ATTITUDES ABOUT ONLINE LEARNING

Course Material Ownership

No matter what the motive, there are a myriad of issues confronting those teaching online. Some of these issues relate to costs and benefits, copyright, ownership, quality, and compensation.

One issue, ownership of course materials, is a particularly sensitive topic since course materials are now more mobile than in the past. Policy recommendations here are not simple since faculty might own course materials but not the courses. In recapping discussion from an invited symposium of higher education leaders, Carol Twigg details a range of potential situations and issues surrounding ownership of online courses and materials.

Her report recommended, "that the default policy position for all institutions should be that the faculty member own the course materials he or she has created." She points out that institutions could have mechanisms in place that spell out situations or conditions wherein a secondary policy would come into play. Faculty in the present study held similar views. Only 16 per cent of faculty members completing this survey agreed that online courses were the property of an institution; 63 per cent disagreed. Keep in mind that this particular survey question concerned courses, not course materials. It is likely that the attitudes would be even stronger in regards to specific course materials. In part, to the fact that only 31 per cent of those responding to the survey indicated that their institution had clear policies regarding ownership of course material. In addition, more than a quarter of those responding to this question were unsure.

As Twigg's report indicated, this is a complex area that higher education institutions need to start addressing more fully so that both faculty and administrators have a clear understanding of university policy on this issue. Despite the lack of clarity regarding ownership of the rights to online courses, more than three-fourths of the faculty members completing this survey indicated that they planned to abide by the ownership guidelines of their home institution, while 19 per cent were unsure if they would. Such responses make it imperative that institutions of higher education clearly state their policies regarding course ownership.

Course Quality

Another commonly debated issue is online course quality. When asked about whether the quality of learning is improved in online environments compared to traditional learning, faculty member opinions were fairly divided. Nearly 40 per cent of the respondents reported that they were unsure, while 32 per cent noted that course quality was, in fact, improved, and another 29 per cent said that it was not.

Such division among early Web adopters is a clear indication that additional research on learning outcomes is needed. As the NEA study points out, those teaching traditionally hold a less positive view of Web-based courses than those actually teaching via distance education. But even among those teaching online, there are some distinct differences of opinion.

Quality of Degrees

As another indicator of faculty views about online course quality, these faculty members were asked about whether they were opposed to bachelor's, master's, and doctoral degrees earned entirely online. Not surprisingly, the responses were less favourable for online doctoral degrees than bachelor's and master's degrees. While around 45 per cent thought that online bachelor's or master's degrees were legitimate, only 29 per cent agreed that doctoral degrees should be available entirely online. For all degrees, the per cent of respondents strongly supporting degrees earned entirely online was under 20 per cent.

Accreditation

Sally Johnstone recently pointed out that many new organizations are emerging to accredit online programmes. However, she also noted that "there are about 100 accrediting bodies that are unrecognized by both the U.S. Secretary of Education and/or the Council for Higher Education Accreditation". Johnstone argues that online education requires speedier responses in terms of accreditation than has been the norm.

As a result, many regional accrediting associations are rethinking and reorganizing their accrediting processes and procedures. In terms of quality, our faculty respondents were believers in the importance of distance education accreditation. In fact, 80 per cent agreed or strongly agreed that accreditation for online distance education is necessary for ensuring academic quality for students.

Perhaps this is not too surprising given the high number of respondents that came from large four-year institutions. We suggest some caution in interpreting these findings, however, since faculty members teaching online at small private universities or at virtual universities may have answered this question quite differently.

Instructor Compensation for Online Teaching

Another major issue, of course, is rewarding faculty who teach online. The traditional publish or perish focus of research-intensive universities forces many young faculty members to avoid pedagogical innovations with technology. Perhaps this accounts for the fact that our sample was older and at higher professorial levels than expected. As cited in Dukart, Lucio Teles argues, "Universities do not have the infrastructure to support online teaching as they do for face-to-face teaching." In terms of compensation, the NEA report showed that distance learning faculty members tend to make comparable wages to those teaching in more traditional settings.

Yet, both sets of faculty members were concerned that they would not be compensated for intellectual property and that they would encounter more work for the same pay. In that study, only 22 per cent of college educators teaching via distance learning received a reduction of course load. Despite these additional burdens, most of those teaching distance learning courses do so voluntarily.

In the present study, instructors were asked how those teaching online should be compensated. One-third indicated that additional salary would be the method of choice. Other answers were fairly equally represented including stipends to spend how they wished, course royalties, and release time. Release time was a common write-in response and would likely have been much higher had it been among the listed options. Awards or recognition was selected by only 4 per cent of the faculty.

Across these answers, some type of monetary commitment is preferred with 63 per cent choosing stipends, royalties, or additional pay. Still, nearly 20 per cent responded that instructors should receive no additional compensation for teaching online courses beyond their normal course pay.

TEACHING AND LEARNING

Teaching and learning should be inseparable, in that learning is a criterion and product of effective teaching. In essence, learning is the goal of teaching. Someone has not taught unless someone else has learned. After a few years of teaching, many faculty realize that students learn too little of what they teach. Science teaching requires attention to both the content of the course and the process of moving students from their initial state of knowledge and understanding to the desired level. In fact, teaching is part of a whole that comprises the teacher, the learner, the disciplinary content, the teaching/learning process, and the evaluation of both the teacher and the learner.

Undergraduate students value good teaching, and many of those who switch from a science major to another field cite poor teaching as an important factor in their decision. When the data from students who persist in a science major was combined with data from students who switched out of a science major, poor teaching by science faculty was the students' most frequently cited concern. Although students are turned off by poor teaching, they also have identified characteristics of good teaching:

- a teacher's enthusiasm and passion for the subject,
- rapport between a teacher and a student or group of students during discussions in and out of class,
- intellectual challenges from a teacher,
- clarity and organization in presenting analytical and conceptual understanding of ideas, and
- a teacher's scholarship.

Teaching Styles

Research indicates that teachers teach in a manner consistent with their own way of learning. However, it is not necessarily true that student learning can be understood from the teachers' own learning history. What is your style of learning? Do you learn most easily if material is presented to you in a formal and structured manner, or do you learn most easily if you are forced to discover basic principles from a series of exercises and examples? Do you believe that your students will learn best if you use a teaching style that helped you learn as a student? Studies of teaching and learning have led to classification of teaching styles into three general categories: discipline-centered, instructor-centered, and student-centered.

In *discipline-centered teaching,* the course has a fixed structure. The needs, concerns, and requirements of teacher and student are not considered because the course is driven by and depends mainly on the disciplinary content that must be presented. The teacher transmits information, but the content is dictated by some separate authority such as a department syllabus committee or textbook author.

The teacher acts as a model of the educated person in *instructor-centered teaching*. He or she is regarded as the authoritative expert, the main source of knowledge, and the focal point of all activity. The student is the passive recipient of the information already acquired by the teacher. The teacher selects from the discipline the information to be taught, studied, and learned.

Student-centered teaching focuses on the student and, in particular, on the cognitive development of the student. The teacher's goal is to help students grasp the development of knowledge as a process rather than a product. The focus of classroom activities and assignments is on the student-centered process of inquiry itself, not on the products of inquiry. Students create their own conceptual or cognitive models. Content, teaching style, and methods are adapted to aid the cognitive and intellectual growth of students. Student-centered teaching combines an understanding of the way that humans process information with other factors that affect learning such as attitudes, values, beliefs, and motivation.

Although there are many ways to teach effectively, all require that the teacher have knowledge of three things: 1) the material being taught; 2) the best instructional strategies to teach the material; and 3) how students learn. New faculty members typically know far more about the content of their discipline than they do about instructional strategies, and therefore tend to use teaching styles similar to those used by their own teachers (Shulman, 1990). In most cases, they use elements of all three general teaching styles. As the teacher gains experience, his or her teaching style is likely to change.

What is the most effective way to teach students? The answer depends on what students are expected to learn. Students taught by lectures, instructor-centered presentations, and student-centered methods achieve similar results on tests that measure factual knowledge. However, student-centered discussions lead to better retention, better transfer of knowledge to other situations, better motivation for further learning, and better problem solving ability. Active participation by students helps them construct a better framework from which to generalize their knowledge.

Developing a Teaching Style

The first step in preparing to teach a particular course is to decide on a particular style of teaching that is compatible with and appropriate for your students and the goals of your course. It is likely that you will use a combination of the three teaching styles, depending on the circumstances of your course. While developing their own teaching style, science teachers must answer a fundamental question: Is the primary goal of my course for each student to gain specific information, or for each student to master how to organize and apply new information independently to new situations? The primary goal may not be the same for each student in a course, especially when the students come from diverse backgrounds. In courses that are the foundation for more advanced learning in a subject area, how should the Bottom of Form

content be organized and presented? Because science curricula tend to be vertically structured, students' content knowledge is critical for advancement in a field and for understanding the next level of information. In science courses for nonscience majors, how should the content be organized and presented? In any given course, we should ask what should be the balance between specific information, application of that information, and conceptual understanding of basic principles? If the course is truly to be a course for lawyers, citizens, teachers, and other nonscientists, it should provide some of the essence of what science is and the nature of the scientific enterprise.

Most science courses, particularly introductory courses, emphasize discipline-centered teaching. Generations of students have been exposed to science as a subject in which the correct formulas and answers must be memorized, and the material is divided into many different and seemingly unrelated pieces. Problems with this approach have been exacerbated by the explosion of scientific information. Faculty members, wishing to cover the latest results and ideas but reluctant to discard classical material, rush to cover more and more information in the same amount of time.

Collaborative Syllabus Design

Often, multiple sections of an introductory course are taught by different faculty members. Some faculty members find it useful to meet with their colleagues to design a syllabus that optimizes the order and structure in which to present the course material. For example, if you are teaching atomic theory, is it best to start with basic terms and then to build up to a model, or to start with a model and disassemble it piece by piece? The first step in collaborative syllabus design is to meet with fellow faculty members who teach the same course to identify basic concepts. Then, separately, each teacher does an analysis of the critical variables related to each concept. Finally, the colleagues reassemble to compare their lists, identify similarities and differences, and discuss the implications of their lists for instruction.

Those who have studied the learning of science have concluded that students learn best if they are engaged in active learning, if they are forced to deal with observations and concepts before terms and facts, and if they have the sense that they are part of a community of learners in a classroom environment that is very supportive of their learning.

Instructor-centered and student-centered teaching are more effective than is discipline-centered teaching for students to learn in this way. When the focus is on meaning rather than solely on facts, students develop their conceptual abilities. They assimilate information by incorporating new concepts or by using information to differentiate among already existing concepts. This is not necessarily at the expense of their development of algorithmic abilities, because conceptual understanding gives a context for the application of problem solving methods. A student-centered style is more likely to motivate students by engaging their interest. Several factors can influence your choice of teaching style:

- student needs (future course and career requirements, preparation for participatory citizenship, and preparation for careers in science, engineering, technology, or education),
- student background,
- familiarity with various teaching methods,
- course enrollment (size, students with special needs, the logistics of managing small group activities),
- student learning styles,
- teaching load (number of contact hours, office hours, time for preparation and grading),
- other responsibilities (research, committee work, administrative duties),
- support structures (equipment cost, teaching and demonstration assistants),
- facilities (laboratory equipment and computers, classroom and laboratory space, and demonstration equipment), and
- parallel sections that require some uniformity of coverage and examination.

In some circumstances, teachers must use methods that emphasize the imparting and acquiring of basic information and skills. Time constraints, class size, or course goals may lead to an emphasis on factual knowledge at the expense of developing a conceptual framework. Students are usually encouraged to accept facts from some authority (e.g., the instructor or the text) without questioning. If all their learning is rote learning, however, students seldom associate the new facts with concepts or models already part of their pictures of the world (A Private Universe, 1989).

What can be done about the many options, goals, and competing pressures? Current practice is not to prescribe one teaching style as best for a given course or type of student. Various methods for engaging students are applied successfully in a wide range of institutional settings.

METHODS OF TEACHING AND LEARNING

The variety of teaching and learning methods which is used within a course is an important ingredient in creating a course with interest to students. A course with a large proportion of its teaching taking place in lectures will need to have a high level of intrinsic interest to students to keep them engaged. Over the past few years, a wide range of different teaching and learning methods have been introduced and tested, often with the aim of developing skills which more didactic methods are poorly adapted to do.

There is a substantial literature on these methods and on how best to use them. It is not possible here to provide great detail on every possible teaching and learning method, so instead we have focused on some of the issues which could be considered by course teams when choosing the components of their course. A useful document to refer to is the Guidelines for Promoting Effective Learning, produced by the Centre for Research on Learning and Instruction and also available in the TLA Centre.

Lectures

Fifty-minute lectures remain the core teaching method for most undergraduate courses. Their role is best suited to providing an overview of the subject matter and stimulating interest in it, rather than disseminating facts. Lecturing to large classes is a skill which not all staff have acquired and some are not comfortable in this role, and so, where possible, a course organiser is advised to try to spread the lecturing load so as to favour those staff with best skill at it, although freedom of action in this respect is often limited!

All students appreciate good quality lectures, and the key ingredients are:

- Clear objectives;
- Clear overhead acetates or slides;
- A paced delivery;

- Appropriate handouts which provide students with complex diagrams or difficult or critical text.

This should not be viewed as spoon feeding. It is part of the process of ensuring that students take away the important elements from a lecture, irrespective of how well the lecture was delivered on the day. Good handouts also help to avoid the communication difficulties which can arise in any lecture where large numbers of students are present.

As class enrolments have risen and lecture theatres are used continuously, ease of access by students to the lecturer at the end of a lecture has been reduced. Providing agreed times and places, as soon as possible thereafter, when they can get questions answered is becoming an important issue. A more radical approach to the problems of the large 'performance' lecture is to consider the extent to which some lectures could be removed entirely and replaced by structured exercises. To some degree, those students who do not attend lectures follow this path anyway!

Tutorials and Seminars

After the lecture, this is probably the next most widely used teaching method. The distinction between what is a tutorial and what is a seminar is woolly - to some it depends upon size whereas to others the seminar has a different structure and different objectives. This last point - objectives - is certainly the most important issue, and it is probably here that most confusion exists in students' minds, and sometimes in tutors' minds too. Clarity of objectives is more important for tutorials than for lectures, in that there is general agreement and expectations for lectures whereas there is certainly greater divergence for tutorials. Much tutorial work is carried out by part-time staff, especially for courses in the first two years, and they too need to be clear about what they are trying to achieve with their students. When asking students about tutorials, the paradoxical finding that they complain about them but ask for more/more frequent tutorials is perhaps closely related to their perception of their need for small group support but lack of clarity about what they should be getting out of what is provided.

Making explicit what students should get out of tutorials can be quite a taxing exercise for the course organiser. A new addition to the tutorial format is that of electronic tutorials via e-mail, sometimes managed in a WWW forum such as HyperNews. Although rather few courses outside those which are traditionally computer-oriented have experimented with these methods, they hold out promise for those courses where students are difficult to bring together or to enable exchanges between face-to-face sessions. The active nature of the tutorial/seminar makes it the main source for students to acquire some of the 'personal transferable skills', *e.g.* in presentation and group work.

Laboratory and Practical Classes

For science subjects, laboratory work is an essential ingredient of the course and some component of this is generally preserved, even though the amount may fall. In addition to the experience of lab work, students often derive a lot of their contact with staff in the lab setting, and compensation for this may be needed if lab time is significantly reduced. High quality lab work is expensive to provide, and it is important that we are sure that students do indeed gain all that they might from it, especially as the number of students present may have increased, more part-time demonstrators are used, and the frills have been trimmed to cut costs. The balance between fewer but better labs and more but simpler is not always easy to find, but is an important consideration.

OTHER TEACHING METHODS

Other methods that may be considered are numerous, including:

- Workbooks, diaries, and lab notebooks;
- Computer-based methods;
- Fieldwork;
- Learning in hospital wards and clinics;
- Independent learning tasks;
- Essays, dissertations and projects;
- Library searches;
- Portfolios;

- Posters;
- Videos.

Judicious use of them gives students the chance to use a variety of learning techniques so that each gets one or more which suits them best. If you find a possible method but are unsure how best to introduce it to your course, search out someone who has used it and pick their brains. You will probably find that TLA Centre can point you to such people, even if they may not be in the University of Edinburgh.

Students With Disabilities

The University has growing numbers of students with disabilities who may present particular challenges to courses with large numbers of students. For example, a profoundly deaf student may be able to follow a lecture with the help of a sign language interpreter, but will not be able to take notes at the same time. A blind student may need special help with practical sessions. It is not possible to give detailed general advice on making the variety of teaching and learning methods described in this manual accessible to disabled students. However, the kind of support which they are likely to find helpful - *e.g.* provision of good handouts - often benefit all students. Students with disabilities are students first and foremost, and in many cases a little thought and ingenuity on the part of lecturing staff is all that is required in order to allow them full benefit from their classes.

Computer Supported Learning

Just as it will be the course organiser's responsibility, in consultation with colleagues contributing to the course, to co-ordinate the availability of resources in the Library all other aspects of resource-based learning will require forward planning with which the course organiser will have to be involved. Various learning technologies are increasingly being used in support of the learning process, presenting new challenges and opportunities for staff and students. A major resource being used more frequently is the World Wide Web. An example of its use in presenting information about course content is given in Case Study 1 at the end of this stage. Wholesale importation of computer-based learning activities across the curriculum is unlikely to be a wise or desirable move for any course. CBL enthusiasts have been predicting significant gains in quality and efficiency of the teaching and learning process for many years, but the realities have, as yet, been less clear cut. On the other hand, computer-based approaches in education have been subjected to more demanding criteria of evaluation than the more traditional approaches have ever had to face. One of the real benefits of the recent interest in new learning technologies has been the reassessment of our more familiar approaches, which has in itself been useful. There are undoubtedly areas of the curriculum, however, in which the appropriate and targeted use of learning technologies will be of considerable importance, affording students the opportunity to engage with materials and resources which would otherwise be impossible.

In particular, the confluence of computer and communication technologies suggest exciting possibilities for the use of computer-mediated communication, in the form of electronic mail or computer conferencing systems, in support of tutorial and group work.

While students are facing increasing financial pressures, with the implication that many are functionally in part-time education, the asynchronous communications with teachers and peers which CMC potentially offers can ease conflict between employment and study. Many subjects, from Fine Art to Neuroanatomy, will benefit from the possibility of networked access to high quality images which may be in short supply, if not completely inaccessible, in the printed form. Computer simulations of practical exercises can allow us to address some of the problems inherent in teaching large classes, provide access to experimental domains which would not otherwise be possible for reasons of cost or personal safety, and circumvent many of the ethical difficulties associated with some areas of research. Many organisations and agencies exist which can provide help to the teacher or course organiser wishing to become involved with the use of IT in the curriculum.

COMPUTER APPLICATION IN EDUCATIONAL INSTITUTIONS

Application Software

Application software is any tool that functions and is operated by means of a computer, with the purpose of supporting or improving the software user's work. In other words, it is the subclass of computer software that employs the capabilities of a computer directly and thoroughly to a task that the user wishes to perform.

This should be contrasted with system software (infrastructure) or middleware (computer services/ processes integrators), which is involved in integrating a computer's various capabilities, but typically does not directly apply them in the performance of tasks that benefit the user. In this context the term application refers to both the *application software* and its implementation. A simple, if imperfect analogy in the world of hardware would be the relationship of an electric light bulb (an application) to an electric power generation plant (a system). The power plant merely generates electricity, not itself of any real use until harnessed to an application like the electric light that performs a service that benefits the user.

Typical examples of 'software applications' are word processors, spreadsheets, media players and database applications. Multiple applications bundled together as a package are sometimes referred to as an application suite. Microsoft Office, OpenOffice.org, and iWork, which bundle together a word processor, a spreadsheet, and several other discrete applications, are typical examples. The separate applications in a suite usually have a user interface that has some commonality making it easier for the user to learn and use each application.

And often they may have some capability to interact with each other in ways beneficial to the user. For example, a spreadsheet may be embedded in a word processor document even though it has been created in a separate spreadsheet application.

User-written software tailors systems to meet the user's specific needs. User-written software include spreadsheet templates, word processor macros, scientific simulations, graphics and animation scripts. Even email filters are a kind of user software. Users create this software themselves and often overlook how important it is. In some types of embedded systems, the application software and the operating system software may be indistinguishable to the user, as in the case of software used to control a VCR, DVD player or microwave oven. It is important to note that this definition may exclude some applications that may exist on some computers in large organizations.

Terminology

The exact delineation between system software such as operating systems and application software is not precise, however, and is occasionally subject to controversy. For example, one of the key questions in the United States v. Microsoft antitrust trial was whether Microsoft's Internet Explorer web browser was part of its Windows operating system or a separable piece of application software. As another example, the GNU/Linux naming controversy is, in part, due to disagreement about the relationship between the Linux kernel and the operating systems built over this kernel. In computer science, an application is a computer programme designed to help people perform a certain type of work. An application thus differs from an operating system (which runs a computer), a utility (which performs maintenance or general-purpose chores), and a programming language (with which computer programmes are created). Depending on the work for which it was designed, an application can manipulate text, numbers, graphics, or a combination of these elements. Some application packages offer considerable computing power by focusing on a single task, such as word processing; others, called integrated software, offer somewhat less power but include several applications.

Application Software Classification

There are many subtypes of application software:

- *Enterprise software* addresses the needs of organization processes and data flow, often in a large distributed environment. (Examples include Financial, Customer Relationship Management, and Supply Chain Management). Note that Departmental Software is a sub-type of Enterprise Software with a focus on smaller organizations or groups within a large organization. (Examples include Travel Expense Management, and IT Helpdesk)

- *Enterprise infrastructure software* provides common capabilities needed to support Enterprise Software systems. (Examples include Databases, Email servers, and Network and Security Management)
- *Information worker software* addresses the needs of individuals to create and manage information, often for individual projects within a department, in contrast to enterprise management. Examples include time management, resource management, documentation tools, analytical, and collaborative. Word processors, spreadsheets, email and blog clients, personal information system, and individual media editors may aid in multiple information worker tasks.
- *Content access software* is software used primarily to access content without editing, but may include software that allows for content editing. Such software addresses the needs of individuals and groups to consume digital entertainment and published digital content. (Examples include Media Players, Web Browsers, Help browsers, and Games)
- *Educational software* is related to content access software, but has distinct requirements for delivering evaluations (tests) and tracking progress through material. It is also related to collaboration software in that many Educational Software systems include collaborative capabilities.
- *Simulation software* are computer software for simulation of physical or abstract systems for either research, training or entertainment purposes.
- *Media development software* addresses the needs of individuals who generate print and electronic media for

others to consume, most often in a commercial or educational setting. This includes Graphic Art software, Desktop Publishing software, Multimedia Development software, HTML editors, Digital Animation editors, Digital Audio and Video composition, and many others.

- *Product engineering software* is used in developing hardware and software products. This includes computer aided design (CAD), computer aided engineering (CAE), computer language editing and compiling tools, Integrated Development Environments, and Application Programmer Interfaces.

Computer Applications

Doctoral programmes are centered around computer graphics and experimental approaches to the design of fractals. Applications have been developed for the design of patterns in carpet and textile industry. Applications have also been developed in discrete dynamical systems. Currently the department is investigating Fractal Theory in improving performance of Fractal Antennas and for noise mitigation in communication systems.

The Department also works in Computer Networking and Wireless Communication with the objective to improve the Quality of Service (QoS) by reducing congestion in high-speed communication. Currently work is in progress in developing new techniques for fast communication after a disaster has occurred.The department has produced five research papers in the last two years: three in international journals and two in national journals. To keep itself abreast of latest developments in computer applications, the Department makes extensive efforts to develop partnerships with industry. We have partnered with IBM to offer an intensive training programme for teachers on 'IT Infrastructure Management' and DB2. We also have collaboration with Infosys under their Infosys Connect Programme to offer intensive training for our students.

The Teaching Learning Process at the MCA level uses the latest electronic teaching aids and is characterized by a tight coupling between lectures, tutorial and laboratory work. The former contributes to interactive classroom learning where the student is able to discuss with the teacher and peer students. The latter enables planned learning and optimization of student teacher time to maximize learning.

Types of Educational Institutions

Computer-Integrated Surgical Systems and Technology Engineering Research Center: Developing novel computing methods, interfacial technologies, and computer-integrated surgical systems to revolutionize surgical procedures in the 21st century.

The impact of Computer-Integrated Surgical Systems and Technology (cisst) on medical care procedures within the next 20 years will be as significant as the impact of Computer-Integrated Manufacturing (CIM) Systems and Technology has been on manufacturing over the past 20 years. A novel partnership between human surgeons and machines, made possible by advances in computing and engineering technology, will overcome many of the limitations of traditional surgery. By extending human surgeons' ability to plan and carry out surgical interventions more accurately and less invasively, Computer Integrated Surgery (CIS) systems will address a vital national need to greatly reduce costs, improve clinical outcomes, and improve the efficiency of health care delivery. Further, the combination of consistent execution, patient and task models, and logging of intraoperative and outcome data made possible by CIS systems will produce the same sort of process learning advantages for surgery that have been realized in semiconductor CIM systems.

3

Technical Support in Online Teaching

Technical support or tech support refers to a range of services by which enterprises provide assistance to users of technology products such as mobile phones, televisions, computers, software products or other electronic or mechanical goods. In general, technical support services attempt to help the user solve specific problems with a product—rather than providing training, customization, or other support services. Most companies offer technical support for the products they sell, either freely available or for a fee. Technical support may be delivered over the telephone or online by e-mail or a website or a tool where users can log a call/incident. Larger organizations frequently have internal technical support available to their staff for computer related problems. The internet is also a good source for freely available tech support, where experienced users may provide advice and assistance with problems. In addition, some fee-based service companies charge for premium technical support services.

Coverage of Support

Technical support may be delivered by different technologies depending on the situation. For example, direct questions can be addressed using telephone calls, SMS, Online chat, Support Forums, E-mail or Fax; basic software problems can be addressed over the telephone or, increasingly, by using remote access repair services;

while more complicated problems with hardware may need to be dealt with in person.

Types of Technical Support

This type of technical support has been very common in the services industry. It is also known as "Break-Fix" IT Support. The concept behind this type of support is that the customer pays for the materials (Hard Drive, Memory, Computer, etc.) as well as pays the technician based on their pre-negotiated rate when they have a problem.

Block Hours

Block Hours is basically a way to purchase a bunch of hours upfront to pay a reduced hourly rate. The premise behind this type of support is that the customer has negotiated a discounted rate and a fixed number of hours to use either per month or year. This allows them the flexibility to use the hours as they please without doing the paperwork and the hassle of paying multiple bills.

Managed Services

Managed Services means a company will receive a list of well-defined services on an ongoing basis, with well-defined "response and resolution times" for a fixed rate or a flat fee. This can include things like 24/7 Monitoring of Servers, 24/7 Help desk for your daily computer issues and On-site visits by a technician when issues cannot be resolved remotely. Some companies also offer additional services like Project Management and Vendor management in the monthly price.

Outsourcing Technical Support

With the increasing use of technology in modern times, there is a growing requirement to provide technical support. Many organizations locate their technical support departments or call centers in countries with lower costs. There has also been a growth in companies specializing in providing technical support to other organizations. These are often referred to as MSP's (Managed Service Providers).

For businesses needing to provide technical support, outsourcing allows them to maintain a high availability of service. Such need may result from peaks in call volumes during the day, periods of high activity due to introduction of new products or maintenance service packs, or the requirement to provide customers with a high level of service at a low cost to the business. For businesses needing technical support assets, outsourcing enables their core employees to focus more on their work in order to maintain productivity. It also enables them to utilize specialized personnel whose technical knowledge base and experience may exceed the scope of the business, thus providing a higher level of technical support to their employees.

Multi-tiered Technical Support

Technical support is often subdivided into tiers, or levels, in order to better serve a business or customer base. The number of levels a business uses to organize their technical support group is dependent on a business' need, want, or desire as it revolves around their ability to sufficiently serve their customers or users. The reason for providing a multi-tiered support system instead of one general support group is to provide the best possible service in the most efficient possible manner. Success of the organizational structure is dependent on the technicians' understanding of their level of responsibility and commitments, their customer response time commitments, and when to appropriately escalate an issue and to which level. A common support structure revolves around a three-tiered technical support system.

Tier/Level 1(T1/L1)

This is the initial support level responsible for basic customer issues. It is synonymous with first-line support, level 1 support, front-end support, support line 1, and various other headings denoting basic level technical support functions. The first job of a Tier I specialist is to gather the customer's information and to determine the customer's issue by analysing the symptoms and figuring out the underlying problem. When analysing the symptoms, it is important for the technician to identify what the customer is trying to accomplish so that time is not wasted on "attempting to solve a symptom instead of a problem." Once identification of the underlying problem is established, the specialist can begin sorting through the possible solutions available. Technical support specialists in this group typically handle straightforward and simple problems while "possibly using some kind of knowledge management tool." This includes troubleshooting methods such as verifying physical layer issues, resolving username and password problems, uninstalling/reinstalling basic software applications, verification of proper hardware and software set up, and assistance with navigating around application menus. Personnel at this level have a basic to general understanding of the product or service and may not always contain the competency required for solving complex issues. Nevertheless, the goal for this group is to handle 70%-80% of the user problems before finding it necessary to escalate the issue to a higher level. In other industries (such as banking, credit cards, mobile telephony, etc.) 1st level support is carried by a call center that operates extensive hours (or 24/7) acting as "initial sink" for user requests and, if required, creating an incident to notify other business teams/units to satisfy user request (provide new pin, blocking stolen credit cards/mobile phones/SIMMs). In some industries, 1st line support actually requires very good knowledge of the products, terms and conditions offered by the business rather than technical information itself (Retail/Wholesale). Most ISPs only offer tier 1 support.

Tier/Level 2(T2/L2)

This is a more in-depth technical support level than Tier I and therefore costs more as the techs are more experienced and knowledgeable on a particular product or service. It is synonymous with level 2 support, support line 2, administrative level support, and various other headings denoting advanced technical troubleshooting and analysis methods. Technicians in this realm of knowledge are responsible for assisting Tier I personnel in solving basic technical problems and for investigating elevated issues by confirming the validity of the problem and seeking for known solutions related to these more complex issues. However, prior to the trouble shooting process, it is important that the technician review the work order to see what has already been accomplished by the Tier I technician and how long the technician has been working with the particular customer. This is a key element in meeting both the customer and business needs as it allows the technician to prioritize the troubleshooting process and properly manage his or her time. If a problem is new and/or personnel from this group cannot determine a solution, they are responsible for raising this issue to the Tier III technical support group. In addition, many companies may specify that certain troubleshooting solutions be performed by this group to help ensure the intricacies of a challenging issue are solved by providing experienced and knowledgeable technicians. This may include, but is not limited to onsite installations or replacements of various hardware components, software repair, diagnostic testing, and the utilization of remote control tools used to take over the user's machine for the sole purpose of troubleshooting and finding a solution to the problem.

Tier/Level 3(T3/L3)

This is the highest level of support in a three-tiered technical support model responsible for handling the most difficult or advanced problems. It is synonymous with level 3 support, back-end support, support line 3, high-end support, and various other headings denoting expert level troubleshooting and analysis methods. These individuals are experts in their fields and are responsible for not only assisting both Tier I and Tier II personnel, but with the research and development of solutions to new or unknown issues. Note that Tier III technicians have the same responsibility as Tier II technicians in reviewing the work order and assessing the time already spent with the customer so that the work is prioritized and time management is sufficiently utilized. If it is at all possible, the technician will work to solve the problem with the customer as it may become apparent that the Tier I and/or Tier II technicians simply failed to discover the proper solution. Upon encountering new problems; however, Tier III personnel must first determine whether or not to solve the problem and may require the customer's contact information so that the technician can have adequate time to troubleshoot the issue and find a solution. In some instances, an issue may be so problematic to the point where the product cannot be salvaged and must be replaced. Such extreme problems are also sent to the original developers for in-depth analysis. If it is determined that a problem can be solved, this group is responsible for designing and developing one or more courses of action, evaluating each of these courses in a test case environment, and implementing the best solution to the problem. Once the solution is verified, it is delivered to the customer and made available for future troubleshooting and analysis.

Tier/Level 4(T4/L4)

While not universally used, a fourth level often represents an escalation point beyond the organization. This is generally a hardware or software vendor. Within a corporate incident management system it is important to continue to track incidents even when they are being actioned by a vendor and the Service Level Agreement (SLA) may have specific provision for this.

Remote PC repair or Remote Computer Repair

Remote PC repair or Remote Computer Repair is a method for troubleshooting software related problems via remote desktop connections. Technicians use software that allows the technician to access the user's desktop via the Internet. With the user's permission, the technician can take control of the user's mouse and keyboard, transfer various diagnostic and repair applications to the user's desktop, run scans, install antivirus programs, etc. If the remote service permits it, the technician can even reboot the PC and reconnect remotely to continue his work without the user needing to assist.

Common repairs available with online computer support providers are computer virus and spyware removal, computer optimization, Windows Registry repair, device driver issues, Web related issues, and Windows security updates. Generally, only software can be "repaired" remotely. A computer with a broken hardware component such as a motherboard or hard disk can in some cases be diagnosed and worked around, but must be repaired in person.

BASIC PRINCIPLES OF TEACHING

In his classic handbook, Teaching Tips, Wilbert McKeachie notes that the unpredictability of teaching both frustrates and fascinates college instructors. You cannot anticipate every eventuality or problem that may pop up during a semester. Understanding and applying a few basic principles of teaching, however, not only will enhance student learning but also make your life as a teacher more rewarding and fun.

Rhythms of the Semester

Much like the rise and fall of the plot in a novel, semester courses unfold in an arc of development. After the flush of excitement during the first week of class, students and instructors begin to settle into more of a routine.

When you think of your own undergraduate courses, you'll recall a definite rhythm to the semester—a brief "honeymoon" period at the beginning when everything seems fresh and exciting; a longer span when students and instructors get to know each other and start establishing patterns of interaction; a stretch about three-quarters of the way into the semester when everyone seems concerned about deadlines, stressed, and, perhaps, ready for a break; and a few weeks before the semester ends, the final push, accompanied, we hope, by a sense of accomplishment.

If you recognize these rhythms, you can design lecture materials, readings, and assignments to fit well with student learning needs at particular points along the continuum. Scheduling all the "fun" learning activities during the first few weeks of the course probably isn't a good idea. On the other hand, waiting until the end of the semester to incorporate "fun" learning might send the message that you've "given up" on helping students work through the final, challenging push of the semester.

Keeping Students Engaged

One of the tenets of American education is that students learn and retain information and skills better if they are actively involved in the learning process. Explain to your students that you expect them to prepare for class, think carefully about course content, take intellectual risks, and participate in class discussion. It is their responsibility to wrestle with the issues and concepts explored in the course; it is your responsibility to support their active involvement with the subject matter. You do this not so much by providing answers as by posing excellent questions.

A substantial literature exists on how students learn and how best to engage them in the learning process. Here are a few tips; many more are available in the Center for Teaching library and online resources.

Lecturing

- If you lecture, remember that research has shown most people actively listen for about 20 minutes. Plan your session accordingly with a break for small-group work, Q&A, or other active learning before resuming the lecture.
- Try to leave the lectern now and then. Walking "into the crowd" will help you make eye contact with students and keep them alert and curious about what you might do next.
- Vary the tone and rhythm of your voice. Use body language effectively.
- Define new vocabulary several times. Avoid jargon.
- Refer to and expand upon material presented in the textbook—don't repeat it.
- Use technology—PowerPoint, film clips, student response systems ("clickers"), tablet PCs, etc.—effectively.
- Speak clearly and at a moderate pace.
- Summarize major points.

Active Learning

- usually involves students in more than listening;
- entails less emphasis on transmitting information and more on developing students' learning and discipline-based skills;
- engages students in higher-order thinking skills such as analysis, synthesis, and evaluation;

- encourages students to explore their own attitudes and values; and
- does not mean you must abandon the lecture format, which is one of several effective ways to convey information.

Active Learning Techniques

- Small-group activities encourage many more students to speak in class. It's harder to be a passive learner in a group of three than in a group of thirty. Small-group activities can be done even in classes of 500 students. All it takes is about five minutes and a well thought-out question or task for groups to work on.
- Effective use of teaching technology can present visual representations via PowerPoint, overhead projectors, videotapes, and tablet PCs. The Center for Teaching and Campus Technology Services can help you incorporate technology in ways that enhance learning and recall of course content and skills.
- Minute papers are easy, fun, and adaptable to many purposes. The goal of this exercise— which can take no more than a minute—is to gather feedback. Minute papers can help you discover what did or did not work well, as well as provide ideas about how to teach in new ways. It can be used in any size class.
- If you are trying to gather general information about what interests or confuses the students or what they think of your teaching, the feedback should be anonymous. Occasionally, you may want to just use the minute paper as a quiz; in that case, of course, names are necessary. Students write for a brief time in response to a focused question from the instructor.

Here are a few examples:

- What is the most important point you've learned in today's class (or this week's readings, this unit, etc.)?
- Did anything confuse you during today's discussion? If so, write it as a question or two.
- What has been the most effective teaching technique used during this unit?

You can do this exercise at any point during the class session, although most instructors do it at the end of a unit or the period. After you've looked through the responses, let students know one or two things you learned and how that information will affect the course. Students are glad to have an opportunity to express themselves in a way that has an impact on their learning in the course.

- Surveys can be conducted several ways, including electronic student response systems ("clickers") and minute papers, anonymous or not. Another effective way to survey students about their opinions or responses to a question is to have them line up along a continuum, discuss their choices, and then ask them to realign themselves along the continuum. If anyone has changed his or her place, ask them to explain why.
- A combination of small-group activities and surveys works well when each group holds up a card to indicate its choice of several answer options. Groups then defend their choices and try to convince others to "join" them.
- Allowing students to jot down a few thoughts before discussing in class can improve the depth of discussion and help those who feel shy about speaking off-the-cuff.
- Board work, role-playing, panel discussions, case studies, posters, and projects also actively engage students by enlisting the fully panoply of learning styles (visual, auditory, reading/writing, and kinesthetic).

Writing

Writing demands critical thinking, organizational skills, patience, and the ability to critique others and to listen to criticism. It's a truism—but also true— that the act of writing forces us to construct our understanding of a topic—in other words, to create as well as to convey meaning.

Writing is one of the essential skills that defines an educated individual, yet teaching writing seems to be the juggernaut of many an otherwise gifted teacher. The following ideas about teaching writing might smooth your way:

- Make writing a regular part of the classroom experience. One-minute papers work well. They can be anonymous or signed. You also can invite students to read aloud what they've written.
- Think carefully about the purpose of the writing assignment:
  - to demonstrate learned knowledge (a quiz or test);
  - to show research abilities—analysis, synthesis, evaluation (term paper);
  - to wrestle with an idea (short essay);
  - to help students speak aloud or focus class discussion (one-minute paper);
  - to help students understand that writing improves thinking (expository writing);
  - to hone communication skills (series of drafts); or
  - to express feelings and opinions, and to reflect on what has been learned, how, and why (personal essay, reflection).
- Design the writing assignment with explicit questions and provide clear learning objectives.
- Invite students to reflect—in writing— on their writing process for any particular assignment and also across the semester.

Even veteran faculty members wonder how to assess written work. Instructors sometimes find assessing personal writing, such as essays or reflections, especially challenging. But simply because a written piece is personal or subjective does not mean it cannot be assessed. A few suggestions to help make assessment of writing effective for your students and efficient for you:

- Help students avoid the temptation to plagiarize by assigning a series of short exercises that build to the final paper or essay.
- Provide written comments in the margins. Marginalia need not be extensive, however, and if you have many students or many short assignments, you can rely on the "check, check-minus, check-plus" technique.

- Writing many comments such as "Good," "Weak," or "Confusing" probably helps the student less than fewer comments that are more specific as to why you find a sentence or paragraph good, weak, or confusing.
- One technique works especially well to start a conversation about written work. Rather than giving students grades for their first draft, ask them to read your comments and then respond. This assignment assures that they actually read and think about your comments. You also can have them rewrite certain sentences, paragraphs, or sections.
- Resist rewriting your students' work—you don't have time and they will not learn if you do the work for them.
- Grammatical errors should not be ignored. On the other hand, you should not serve as a copy editor for your students. Undoubtedly, they have been told about run-on sentences, "their" vs. "there," and misspelled words many times before. What to do?
    - Put check marks in the margins and tell students to find and correct the errors on the marked lines.
    - Mark and correct one paragraph and tell them to find identical errors and fix them in the rest of the piece.
    - Tell students they will be exchanging papers for peer review of grammar and usage.
- Devote some time throughout the semester to teaching a few of the most frequent—and egregious—examples of bad grammar and usage. These exercises can be amusing, and students almost always appreciate learning or brushing up on a few basic writing skills.
- Develop and use a rubric for grading writing. Be sure to hand it out to students at the same time as you give them the assignment so they know what is expected of them. Writing assessment rubrics generally cover nuts-andbolts such as grammar and usage, but also include content, organization, critical thinking skills, and stylistic considerations.

Service Learning

Today, many students come to college having already performed impressive volunteer work in their communities. They are eager to participate in volunteer and service-learning opportunities in college.

Service-learning courses provide active learning experiences by integrating community service with academic course work. Service learning requires students to apply what they learn in class in their community service efforts and then bring their volunteer experiences to bear on their classroom learning. As a teaching assistant in a service-learning course, you may be helping the faculty instructor and students establish community partnerships. You also may be monitoring and helping to assess the service aspect of the course, and possibly even engaging in community service yourself.

Teaching in Laboratory or Studio Settings

- Students who take lab or studio courses necessarily engage in active learning. In these types of courses, teaching assistants work with students on a more individual basis. To enhance the lab or studio experience:
- Introduce the conceptual background for their activities in each session of the lab or studio.
- Inform them of what they are going to do and the learning objectives for the activities.
- Make certain you have already conducted the experiment, or, in a studio, are familiar with the materials and media being used. Point out where you had difficulties and how you resolved them.
- Circulate around the room as students work. Ask them what they're doing and why and to interpret their results.
- Ask them to link what they are doing at the moment to what has been learned in the classroom or through the textbook.
- Invite questions.
- Remind students about safety issues and where to find devices and individuals to help in an emergency.

Effective use of Technology

At one time, slate blackboards were considered "cutting-edge" technology. But an instructor who wrote on the blackboard with his back to students was not using this technology in a way to optimize student learning. Incorporating technology into a course should not be an end unto itself, but a way to broaden and enhance learning. Although there are excellent pedagogical reasons to use technology to teach, many students—including graduate student TAs—have experienced "death by PowerPoint" or comparable technology faux pas. Any technology—even blackboards— risk becoming the end rather than a means for better teaching and learning.

Nevertheless, many excellent reasons exist for incorporating technology such as PowerPoint, student response systems, tablet PCs, ICON (course development and management systems), and videotapes in the teaching process. The Center for Teaching and Campus Technology Services help TAs and faculty members effectively incorporate technology into their teaching. The center assists with pedagogy, while Campus Technology Services can help with any technical issues.

Assessment of Learning

The most obvious way to assess student learning is by graded assignments or exams. However, many other assessment techniques exist to help you and your students understand their mastery of knowledge and skills.

For instance, one-minute papers can reveal much about what students learned during one class session and what might confuse them. Discussion, small-group work, class surveys, written reflections, periodic questionnaires, and self-evaluation of learning also help both instructor and students determine where they stand in terms of learning content and developing a facility with required skills.

Grading

Assigning grades can be an angst-filled time for TAs. Finding out the answers to these questions may help you feel more at ease in the grading process:

- How much responsibility do I have for assigning particular or overall grades?
- Am I following my supervising faculty member's instructions on grading, including adhering to the grading schedule?
- Does my department have a grading curve that I am supposed to use in the course?
- Does my department or the course faculty instructor employ a rubric for grading particular assignments or exams? If so, when will I provide it to students?
- Will other TAs and the course faculty instructor discuss standards and expectations for grading? Will TAs calibrate their grades via a practice grading exercise?
- How will I handle the grading of students for whom English is a second language?
- What is the departmental, course supervisor's, or my policy on makeup exams and late assignments?

Your course supervisor or department may dictate grading guidelines, although you may have discretion in assigning at least some percentage of grades in a course.

While some departments require that all student work be graded, others encourage a variety of approaches to learning assessment, including observations and comments by instructors throughout the semester with grades only assigned at the end of the term. Instructors are not required to employ pluses or minuses on grades.

The clearer you are about how you will assign grades prior to the actual grading process, and the better records you keep, the more likely you can avoid grade disputes later.

TAs who serve as graders for a professor should receive clear instructions about how to evaluate subjective responses. If more than one TA works with one class, the assistants and professor should meet to hammer out consistent grading standards. TAs also can rehearse and calibrate their grading.

During this process, TAs review identical exam answers or papers, compare the responses and grades they would have assigned, and discuss differing reactions member then develop a rubric that specifies the criteria everyone will use to evaluate student work.

Grades, of course, can be a source of friction between students and instructors. Students want to know that instructors have been consistent and fair in their grading. The following points will help you achieve consistency and fairness and demonstrate your commitment to those qualities should a student question his or her grade:

- Keep accurate and duplicate copies of your grading records.
- Maintain records that can be easily interpreted by your supervising faculty member.
- Inform students fairly often throughout the semester about their progress in the course. This does not need to be a grade, but it should be evaluative in some way.
- Create a rubric (or a scoring guide that assigns specific points to each answer) when grading papers or exams.
- After you've developed a rubric or scoring guide, "test" it by applying it to five or ten exams or papers. If your grading guidelines don't seem reasonable, alter them.
- After you have graded all the exams or papers, reexamine the first few that you graded. Are the standards you applied at the beginning of the grading process the same as the standards you used at the end?
- When evaluating written work, try to find at least one thing to praise and encourage further work. And even students who produce "A" writing need to be given new, higher goals to shoot for.
- Make clear that you have considered what a student is trying to say in written work as well as how they have managed to communicate it.

Attendance

The University's Operations Manual defines excused and

reported absences. You must allow work and exams to be made up if a student misses class because of an excused absence. Excused absences include absences due to participation in a school-sanctioned athletic or other event for which the student has provided prior notice of event dates.

Large-scale tragedies or unexpected events can affect many students and their instructors. Research has shown that students appreciate instructors who acknowledge the event and provide an opportunity to discuss it and its impact during class time. Such consideration by instructors reinforces the shared sense of community among students. Whether during the current class session or the next session, turning back to the course work at hand after thoughtful discussion can provide a welcome return to normal routine.

Communicating with your students:

- You will communicate with your students through a variety of technological means and in a variety of venues. Planning ahead about how to communicate effectively can help avoid potential pitfalls in communication later.
- The syllabus should include the TA office or at least the departmental telephone number. It is up to you whether you provide your home telephone number to students.
- ICON offers many opportunities for communication, such as chat rooms, threaded discussions, feedback surveys, and more.
- TAs can make creative use of their time during office hours. To become familiar with your students and help ease them into the course, you might schedule individual conferences with them during the first month of the course. As the semester continues, you might also use office hours to host small-group workshops or reviews.
- Email is a popular way for students to communicate with instructors, and instructors sometimes incorporate online discussion via email as a course requirement.
- Most students are familiar with email before arriving on campus and all students may sign up for a free email

account through the University. The process is included in the ISIS sign-on. Nevertheless, many students prefer to use another account, so if you want a list of your students' email accounts, you should ask them to email you and save their addresses in your email address book.

- The course planning and management system ICON also has email capabilities, including a method to send to the entire class.
- Include your email address and hours in your syllabus, as well as your expectations for email communication. Inform students that you are not available via email (or otherwise) except during certain hours, and that they cannot expect you to respond immediately.
- The Family Educational Rights and Privacy Act of 1974 (FERPA) generally prohibits disclosing educational records (including grades) to anyone other than the student or a university official with a legitimate educational need to view the record. Instructors communicating via email about grades need to be certain they are, indeed, communicating with the students. In general, sending an email to a student's University address or via ICON provides adequate assurance that the recipient is the student. Emailing to another address such as gmail or AOL does not provide adequate assurance.
- Some instructors accept assignments as attachments, and some do not due to potential viruses or system incompatibility. Indicate in your syllabus whether you will accept assignments via email attachment.
- Be alert to the possible risks of communicating via email, in particular, the challenges of interpreting intent and tone online. Irony and light sarcasm can be devastating to a student. Maintain a friendly, but professional tone and focus, and insist your students do the same. Write your messages with the assumption that your supervisor or department chair will read them.
- If you encounter the rare electronic message that is inappropriate, hostile, or bullying, forward it immediately

to your faculty supervisor. If your supervisor feels you should respond, maintain professional integrity, copy your supervisor, and let the student see that you have done so.

- Save all messages and make paper copies for your course file.

OBSTACLES TO WEB-BASED TEACHING SUPPORT

There certainly are a myriad of obstacles to utilizing the Web in higher education instruction. Issues of time, training, experience, ownership, costs, confidence, technological infrastructure, administrative support, and interest are often mentioned. In this study, the main obstacle to effective use of the Web was time; more specifically, the amount of preparation time required for Web-based course development and delivery. Sixty per cent of the college instructors in this survey reported that preparation time was a major issue. What other obstacles did our respondents face? Contrary to findings from the NEA study, nearly 4 in 10 found the lack of technical support to be a major deterrent.

Slightly fewer, 37 per cent, indicated that a lack of time to learn to use the Web was an obstacle. Along these same lines, a quarter of the respondents lacked training on how to use the Web. And even if they did receive proper training or time allocation, nearly 30 per cent felt that they lacked the equipment or software to display the Web in the classroom. Of course, such findings contrast with what was reported earlier about fairly abundant technology access. Perhaps it indicates that technology is available in their buildings for utilizing the Web in instruction, but it is not yet found in their particular classroom settings.

What were not viewed as major obstacles? Fewer than 20 per cent of the faculty respondents cited lack of hardware or outdated equipment in their office as a barrier. Even fewer, 15 per cent, indicated that the lack of software or outdated software was a problem. And amazingly, fewer than 2 per cent had no interest in using the Web in their teaching. Keep in mind, once again, that the respondents were generally early Webbased teaching adopters who would be expected to be interested in using the Web in their instruction.

Still, the nearly unanimous interest in using the Web indicates that this is a technology with the potential for transforming higher education. Around 17 per cent of the respondents remarked on other problems holding up their adoption of the Web in their teaching. In open-ended responses, these early Web adopters focused on issues of administrative support, time, student interest, pedagogy, vision, funding, incentives, utility, reliability, motivation, and bandwidth.

Administrative support comments included:

- "Lack of administrative vision."
- "Lack of incentive from administration and the fact that they do not understand the time needed."
- "Lack of system support."
- "Little recognition that this is valuable."
- "Rapacious intellectual property policy."
- "Unclear university policies concerning intellectual property."

Pedagogical comments included:

- "Difficulty in performing laboratory experiments online."
- "Impossible to teach drawing and lithography."
- "Lack of appropriate models for pedagogy in content-based instruction."

Time-related comments included:

- "Lack of incentive."
- "More ideas than time to implement."
- "Not enough time to correct online assignments."
- "People need sleep; Web spins forever."
- "Time to grade/interact."

Cost also appears to be an issue as the following comment notes, "Institution supports because it is the cheapest...is too hard for students and faculty to learn." The following comment from one respondent summarizes many of these issues:

- "...(the) lack of time to develop materials and add to what is already developed. Little recognition that this is valuable and thus hurts promotion and tenure decisions which seem to be primarily based on publications in juried journals not on stuff on the Web."

When comparing obstacles encountered at private and public institutions, two important differences emerged,

1. The perceived lack of time to learn to use the Web and
2. Other obstacles faced by faculty at private institutions.

First, faculty members from public institutions were significantly more likely to indicate that time to learn to use the Web was a problem than those from private institutions. It is unclear, however, whether this is due to differing teaching and research expectations, support structures, or Web-based learning initiatives at their institutions.

Second, 30 per cent of the faculty respondents from private universities noted that they faced other obstacles not listed as compared to just 14 per cent of respondents from public institutions. On several other items, faculty members from public institutions were more likely to indicate problems than those from private ones. For instance, faculty respondents from public institutions were slightly more likely to complain that Web-based learning required too much preparation time and that they lacked the proper equipment to display the Web in their classrooms.

An interesting finding emerged when comparing differences in the number and type of obstacles by the size of the institution. While faculty respondents from smaller institutions perceived a lack of Web training, computer hardware, and technology support compared to those from larger institutions, only the perceived lack of support for technical problems and courseware development was significantly different.

More specifically, 47 per cent of those from institutions under 3,000 students viewed this as a problem, 53 per cent of those from institutions between 3,000 and 9,999 noted it as a major obstacle, and only 31 per cent from institutions over 10,000 indicated that this was an obstacle. When combining the responses for those in institutions under 10,000 students, the differences remained significant with 51 per cent of those in the smaller institutions indicating a need for such technical and courseware support versus only 31 per cent in larger institutions.

There were also some modest indications that the lack of Web training and inadequate technology in the classroom and office were also obstacles in the smaller colleges and universities. We also explored obstacles to Web-based teaching as reported by gender. The only item that approached a significant difference here was a lack of software or outdated software that was noted by 19 per cent of the males compared to only 9 per cent of the females. However, females pointed to such obstacles as time to learn to use the Web, lack of classroom equipment to display the Web, too much preparation time, and a lack of technical and courseware development support. Apparently, there are more perceived barriers for female instructors in college settings than for males.

While male instructors might recognize outdated software tools, females seem to be seeking additional training and support. Overall, time for course preparation and delivery as well as technical and administrative support are among the major obstacles for college instructors attempting to teach online. Equipment and software tools are less significant factors. All findings vary, however, by type and size of institution.

Support for Web-Based Teaching and Research

The survey also addressed the type of support required by college educators to utilize the Web in their teaching, research, and administrative duties. Given the previous answers regarding online teaching obstacles, it was not surprising that release time was the most popular form of support selected here.

In addition, each of the following three forms of support were desired by nearly 7 in 10 respondents:

1. Recognition for use of the Web in tenure, promotion, and salary review decisions;
2. Technical support staff to assist with online course development and associated technical problems; and

3. Instructional development grants or stipends.

Given the lack of differentiation in responses, universities may want to embed aspects of a few of these key support preferences in their distance education policies and initiatives. For instance, they might offer options between release time, instructional development grants and stipends, additional salary, and designated technical support. They might also adopt policies and practices wherein online teaching and research activities would be more fully recognized in college professor tenure and promotion cases. Nearly 60 per cent of respondents felt that it would be valuable for instructional designers to assist faculty members when needed. The same per cent asked for time to learn about and utilize the Web. In addition, 45 per cent thought that additional training on how to use the Web in teaching would be beneficial.

Around thirty per cent of these faculty respondents suggested that greater student access to computers as well as online resources would also be helpful, while slightly over one fourth of them considered e-mail notification of technology changes or updates to be valuable. In contrast, a mere 13 per cent thought that chat room help for Web-related problems was a support they needed for effectively using the Web in teaching, research, or administrative duties.

A few respondents suggested additional ideas for online teaching support. Among the advice was for "better equipped classrooms for demos," "really specific examples of 'good courses' so we have some idea what we are trying to achieve," "more money," and "assistance with routine office tasks, grading objective tests, etc., to free up my time to create Web lectures and other course materials." Others argued for outcome data and useful learning research, clearer royalty definitions, and administrators who believed in the priorities of student learning and could articulate the importance of Web teaching.

These support needs correspond closely with the perceived obstacles including the need for greater technical support. Given these findings, it appears that a multi-pronged approach to online instructor support and training is warranted. Respondents at public and private institutions expressed some significant differences in the types of support they needed.

Those in public institutions were significantly more likely to ask for online resources to use the Web effectively in their teaching, research, and administrative duties compared to those in private institutions. They were also significantly more likely to suggest that they needed instructional development grants or stipends to support their online teaching efforts than those at private institutions. Along these same lines, they were significantly more inclined to ask for release time than those in private institutions. Perhaps faculty members at public institutions are simply more demanding.

For instance, other areas wherein faculty members in public institutions indicated that they needed more support to effectively use the Web in their scholarly pursuits than those in private institutions included the need for instructional design help, time to learn about and utilize the Web, greater training regarding how to use the Web in teaching, greater access to computers for students, and recognition for tenure, promotion, and salary review decisions.

Technical support staff was identified as necessary by about 68 per cent of both public and private institution respondents. It is clear that those in public institutions have higher expectations of the support structures required before adopting the Web in their teaching and other duties. Whether they have differing instructional standards, course loads, or support histories and experiences is not known and is an open question for further investigation. In exploring the data by size of institution, there were no significant differences in Webbased teaching support.

However, from a descriptive standpoint, faculty members at institutions with enrollments under 3,000 students pointed to the need for instructional design support and training on how to use the Web in teaching. Instructors in medium-sized institutions were more likely to select time to utilize the Web and student access to computers. Instructors at the medium and large institutions favoured recognition for tenure, promotion, and salary review decisions, development grants and stipends, and release time.

While none of these differences were significant, they do

provide an interesting picture of Web-based teaching support needs at different sized institutions. When comparing those in institutions larger and smaller than 10,000 students, respondents at the smaller colleges and universities were more likely to select technical support and student access to computers as important issues, whereas instructors at the large institutions were focused on having more online resources, recognition, and development grants or stipends. Gender differences in terms of perceived supports were minimal.

CREATE A STRUCTURE FOR ONLINE TECHNICAL SUPPORT

The Distance Learning Committee should be diversely comprised of administrators, faculty, and staff to guide and direct the effort. The committee must decide what the overall mission and goals are for the Distance Learning Program and ensure that these are consistent with an Institution's mission and values. With particular regard to the technical support portion of the Distance Learning Plan, the committee will define what services, processes and protocols are needed by students accessing information online; determine what staff and technologies are needed to provide these services, and in doing so they will create the necessary jobs and outline individual roles; and, create/request/establish a budget and policy that reflects a commitment to the program.

FORMATIVE SERVICES AND/OR PROCESSES

The committee should think what information systems and technology are currently available to the students and what systems/technology will be made available in the near future (near future meaning whatever timeframe the committee establishes for periodically reviewing services for changes/ upgrades). Looking at each system or technology, the committee must establish the nature of the technical support that students will need. The committee should develop a plan and timeline to determine what services should be offered as a first critical level of operations, and what services will be necessary in a second or, if necessary, a third stage, level, or phase.

Any consideration of technical support should take into

consideration the institution's existing online support services, as well as existing technical support services offered on campus. The strengths and weaknesses of the services should be evaluated to isolate areas that could be used or strengthened to provide a foundation for the technical support services needed online. To be effective, technical support personnel should work closely with staff involved with online student services in areas such as the library, campus book store, financial aid, and other student support departments.

Some of the technical support services wanted will be out of the scope of current resources with regards to staff, software/ hardware tools, and budget. Consideration should be given to alternatives, remembering that not all services must be provided internally. In order to evaluate whether or not it is more cost effective to outsource these services or provide them indigenously, a cost benefit analysis should be developed and implemented, along with some type of checklist, matrix, model, or form to be used as a guide. An example of this type of analysis is provided by *Beyond the Administrative Core: Creating Web Based Student Services for Online Learners* (2003).

Things to consider when evaluating the feasibility of building, buying, or partnering:

- Do we currently own or have access to staff with the necessary ability, and/or technology with the functionality to provide this service?
- Is there a possible partnership that will provide a solution?
- If building, what is the estimated development time, in hours?
- If buying, what additional costs are involved? Consider training, upgrades, maintenance, annual fees, and technical support.
- If buying, what is the scalability? Customizability? Usability? Reliability?
- Whether building, buying, or partnering is security a concern?

Finally, the priority order of any new services under

consideration will need to be established. It is a good idea to get input from all stakeholders to determine whether existing services are adequate or need improvement, and what new services are needed or desired.

Faculty will be invited and encouraged to attend committee meetings. Student surveys can be conducted with the cooperation of the offices of Student: Services, Activities, Engagement, and/or Success. The expectation here is that the open communication and the implementation of surveys provide constructive feedback and prompt proposals that will ensure continued growth and overall ongoing process improvement.

Assess Technical Needs

The Distance Learning Committee must ensure that the technologies used to deliver instruction are appropriate for students and curriculum while striving to assure a consistent technological framework. The policy process should assure that institutional instructional guidelines are met in this online environment with the appropriate technology to fulfill these guidelines.

Here are some important considerations when assessing technology needs:

- What are the minimum hardware and software requirements and are they practical?
- What forms of online interaction and communication will be encouraged or supported? (Ex: chat, email, Blogs, bulletin boards)
- Can/will we provide support for multiple platforms?
- Are we meeting ADA requirements?
- Are there any concerns regarding security? When and where?
- How will requests for specialized software be handled?
- What plug-ins and viewer downloads will be required?
- Is software licensing an issue?

Generate Jobs and Define Roles

Questions to consider when creating jobs and identifying staff roles are:

- Who will provide leadership?
- Who will provide training?
- Who will provide the administrative/clerical support?
- Who will provide the end-user technical support?

In some cases this will be one multi-talented individual with a complex role and diverse responsibilities, but in others a dedicated member of staff will be necessary in each of these individual roles.

The Distance Learning initiative requires the committee to appoint a team leader, facilitator, project coordinator, or director to provide leadership. Although the skills and abilities will be dependant on the unique needs of each institution, this person should possess an overall understanding of technology while demonstrating the ability to be creative and innovative when facing limited resources.

The Distance Learning leader and team will advise and collaborate with the training staff to establish the baseline for minimum training requirements and objectives; develop a review procedure to evaluate the baseline; designate any changes or updates needed; and implement a process to adjust the training requirements accordingly. Technical support training should be conducted using a variety of media to allow for reasonable access with regard to ADA issues and technological restrictions such as low bandwidth or limited access to the Internet. Various types of presentation should be used to maximize attendance and allow for different learning styles. The best practice is to offer the user a variety of options for training: face-to-face sessions, printable materials, and an option for self-paced learning. Self-paced learning is also beneficial to those learners who may not need a review of the entire subject but one particular task or area of study. The Distance Learning Committee will determine administrative and end-user support staffing and technology needs based on services determined to be required for a viable online technical support system.

Demand Funds or Create a Budget

A financial plan must be in place in order to assure the

acquisition of technology (both hardware and software) and staffing support. The budget must be sufficient to fulfill the minimum requirements of a viable online technical support system. The Committee will develop a long term budget plan that will take into consideration the processes, staffing, and technology needs of each service; determine where we are now as an enterprise; and map-out the direction that should be taken with future initiatives.

Encourage Awareness

The Distance Learning Committee, in agreement with the technical support services leadership, will need to include a plan for promoting awareness of these online technical support services. Collaboration with the Public Relations department or an equivalent institutional area responsible for promotion of campus services and/or events should be a priority. The support of the entire college community is critical to assure success. Every opportunity must be taken advantage of to showcase these services to faculty, staff, and students accessing information online. Schedule time within the Student and/or Freshman Orientation sessions, Faculty Convocations, and Staff Development events to promote awareness, demonstrate services, and issue training schedules. Develop flyers, brochures, presentations, and electronic media of various types (CDs, emails, newsletters, and/or websites) to promote services offered. Along the lines of promoting awareness, the committee should seek to incorporate the technical support module into the institution's existing online support services. Again, collaboration with Online Student Services offered through other institutional areas such as the Library/Media Services, Financial Aid, Admissions & Records, Campus Bookstore, Advising and/or Counseling is critical for the highest level of exposure to members of the campus and community. Student labs are another valuable resource for promoting student services.

Technology – The I. T. Connection

A web presence is essential for providing any service online. A Distance Learning website will serve as the gateway to contact information, a link to a simulated classroom environment, internal and external learning resources, and Help Desk support. To ensure proper/desirable usability and navigability all of the essential resources should have a link on the main page that provides access to online support and secondary resources listed in sub pages. Hyperlinking to established campus student services already provided online will foster increased cooperation between institutional resources.

Best practices in overall web design should be followed. For a quick look at some best practices, you can use Grantastic Design's *The 5 Basic Rules of Web Page Design and Layout* or a little more in-depth look at best practices can be found at *The Programmer in Black*website. There is even a site for anyone wanting to know what NOT to do when designing your site. It's called *Web Pages that Suck*.

More information on usability is available at *Usability*. A usability guide can also be found at *The World Wide Web Consortium* website with a shorter version found at *All Things Web. A*nother good resource is *Usableweb*.

Contact information should include any available operating hours, phone numbers, email addresses, physical addresses, and location information for designated support staff as well as faculty teaching online courses. Be sure to provide any building, room number, and maps where possible. Distance Learning course information can be included here or accessible via a link to the faculty, discipline, or other instructional webpage containing this information. Post a guide that is both easy to find and easy to read that tells who to contact, when (for what services), and how best to contact for expedited service.

Frequently Asked Questions (FAQ's) should be made readily available to help the student do as much troubleshooting as possible before contacting technical support. This empowers the student as much as it helps free up the technical support assistance. Technical requirements and the opportunity to submit your troubleshooting tips should be available here. In cases where FAQ's are plentiful, using categories, an index, or search features will save time and curb frustration. Both internal and external technical resources available should be utilized to create the best possible online technical support service. Also, on this website should be links to related online support services available from the institution (for example, Library/Media Services, Financial Aid, Admissions & Records, the Bookstore, Advising and/or Counseling) with a summary of the online services each provides.

Investigate external resources to cover or enhance those needs your institution is currently lacking or that are nonexistent due to limited resources. For example: a request is made for a graphical calendar displaying the training events but you do not have the hardware/software to provide this service indigenously - *Calendars Net* is a free interactive web calendar hosting service that will allow you to provide this service with the minimum requirement of designating a staff member to maintain the events.

Technical support for students should always involve examining the classroom learning environments and technologies they will be using that includes a demonstration of the tasks they will be expected to perform. This experience should provide the student with a good idea of what the limitations and/or criteria are for each of the tasks they may be asked to do. An excellent way to give the Distance Learning student the experience of learning online in a safe and controlled environment is to set up a simulated classroom using each technology available to the faculty. The activities demonstrated in simulated classrooms should be accessible in a real-time capacity for face-to-face instruction, in a printable format for review, and in a presentation format such as PowerPoint. The software used to create the presentation is not as important as the interactivity. A limited example of every classroom activity available to the faculty should be demonstrated here along with a hands-on portion where students can apply what they've learned. Some of these presentation forms will allow the student to access this training whether using the Internet, an intranet, any virtual networks available, CD, or DVD.

Although some students find taking a class online best fits their schedule or lifestyle, there are students with limited resources or access to technology outside of school. For this reason students will use the college labs to access their classroom and complete their homework so it is important to include the student labs when considering how to best way to deliver training materials.

Training information should be a high priority link accessible within one click. The schedule for any face-to-face training available to the campus community should be prominently displayed and easy to find. Options for submitting a request for training materials or a face-to-face session should be available as well. Clearly outline the registration process or procedure for training sessions along with any other information regarding user requirements. Whether listed as a part of this site or as links to partner websites, tutorials and other learning materials should be available from this website. These could be, for example, links to the Blackboard, Vista (or other course technology tool) support center for students or a link to online tutorials for using a Microsoft Office product such as Microsoft Word. Tutorials can be provided in-house or by other partner institutions and websites such as *Education Online for Computer Software*.

The Help Desk is a complex technical support tool and should be approached in phases using the aforementioned feasibility analysis process/procedure/matrix. The first phase should start with the basic structure of phone support from a minimum of 8am to 5pm and with a goal of 24/7 telephone coverage. Initially, a website can be used for technical support after hours posted on the website as FAQ's, troubleshooting tips, and tutorials. The website should also outline the steps a user needs to take to get help. These steps should be prominently displayed; as clear and easy to read as possible; and should define whom to call and when. The telephone coverage together with a web presence should provide a good foundation but should be re-evaluated periodically by the Distance Learning Committee to determine needs for growth. The evaluation process should be developed by the Distance Learning Committee and established prior to the implementation of the Help Desk services.

4

Online Education and Technology

Studying along with working has become quite a common trend among the young generation these days. Unlike the past education system, where pupil are required to visit their respective colleges and universities and attend the classes, the modern generation depends on online education. We are grateful to the technological advancements that we are able to reap a long list of benefits in this epoch. Keeping pace with the fast and competitive world, students cannot afford to send two or three years concentrating only on studies. Instead they prefer to do any job and continue with their education. The Scope of Online Education seems ever increasing. Since the advent of this type of education, it has been able to attract a large percentage of student population all over the world.

When it comes to secure the Scope for Online Education, one must consider the fact that online education is not limited to only one country and institution. This is considered an education without boundaries, which allows the students to study their chosen subjects at their ease. The Scope of Online Education is widening since more and more universities are offering distance courses on each and every subject you want to pursue. The students all over the world are resorting to this type of education as they get absolutely all the convenience they can expect to get. The choices offered by universities across the world are worth appreciating.

Leaving behind the traditional method of studying, students are becoming more inclined in adopting convenient methods of going about. Since there is an all round growth in the field of online education, most of the interested students are opting for this. Starting from Online Masters Degree and Bachelor Degree to Online Doctorate Degree and Short-term Diploma & Certificate Courses, the Scope of Online Education is increasing to a great extent. Although this online education system was initially developed in the European countries, gradually countries of different continents are also keeping pace with that. Breaking the national boundaries, students can look forward to get education for the reputed universities all over the world. Keeping in mind the convenience of the students, majority of educational institutions are launching their websites and offering multiple range of courses to the brilliant and interested.

Owing to the fact that people are becoming more used to internet and they have access to internet, the scope for Online Education gets widened. The willing students who look forward to go for international education can surely count on this. Unlike the initial online education, the students are always able to choose from a variety of subjects which are not always found on all the universities. In the modern times Scope of Online Education has increased to a wide extent. With the growing popularity of online education the facilities offered by the reputed colleges and universities have increased. This online education is opening up the option for the students worldwide and enables the students to interact with a large number of other people related to that subject which you are pursuing.

IMPORTANCE OF EDUCATIONAL TECHNOLOGY

In the past, learning and education simply meant face-to-face lectures, reading books or printed handouts, taking notes and completing assignments generally in the form of answering questions or writing essays. In short; education, learning and teaching were considered impossible without a teacher, books and chalkboards. Today, education and training have taken on a whole new meaning. Computers are an essential part of every classroom and teachers are using DVDs, CD-ROMs and videos to show students how things work and operate. Students can interact with the subject matters through the use of such web based tools and CD-ROMs. Moreover, each student can progress at his/her own pace.

How Important is Technology in Education

The role of technology in the field of education is four-fold: it is included as a part of the curriculum, as an instructional delivery system, as a means of aiding instructions and also as a tool to enhance the entire learning process. Thanks to technology; education has gone from passive and reactive to interactive and aggressive.

Education is essential in corporate and academic settings. In the former, education or training is used to help workers do things differently than they did before. In the latter; education is geared towards creating curiosity in the minds of students. In either case, the use of technology can help students understand and retain concepts better.

Factors that Help Students Learn Better

Research has shown, time and again, that students learn best when they are engaged. Through the use of technology, students can become active participants as opposed to passive ones where they simply receive instructions or information. Trust is another factor that enhances the learning ability of students.

With the help of technology, teachers can establish credibility in what they are teaching. Web based tools can be used for providing demonstrations and examples that can help students establish credence in what they are learning.

Technology Allows Distance Learning

Perhaps the greatest impact of technology in the field of learning is its ability to help several people learn simultaneously from different locations. Learners are not required to gather at a predetermined time or place in order to learn and receive instructions and information. All one needs is a computer connected to a modem (or with a CD drive); these tools can literally deliver a 'classroom' in the homes and offices of people.

Technology Allows Group Learning

There are naysayers who argue that distance learning of this sort cannot help students receive the support of traditional group-based learning. For proving this theory wrong, technology has helped provide distance learners with online communities, live chat rooms and bulletin boards. All these allow students to collaborate and communicate even though they are isolated in their own space.

Technology Allows Individual Pacing

Multimedia tools, on-line and CD-ROM based training have helped eliminate the need for an instructor-based lesson plans. Students who grasp concepts faster proceed and move along, without being held back by ones who need more time and help for learning. Such individual pacing is beneficial to all.

Technology Helps Lower Training Costs and Increases Productivity

Another benefit of using technology to reach many students in shorter time is lowering training costs. Corporate and academic Institutions can reduce their costs of delivering lessons to students on a per-student basis. Moreover, technology produces quantifiable results and allows students to put into practice this information quickly and with better results. Through the use of technology, students can considerably save time and increase their productivity. Both these points justify the higher costs of advanced technological tools.

Roadblocks in the Use of Technology in Learning

Naturally, for education technology to have a positive impact on students, it should be designed and prepared well. Tools used for disseminating information must be developed with students in mind. There are also factors like lack of computer/technology literacy to be considered. Schools and businesses must bear in mind that education technology is simply a tool and its success depends largely on the amount of planning that goes into it. Using education technology can be a right choice as long as all such factors are considered.

CRITICISM OF EDUCATIONAL TECHNOLOGY

Although technology in the classroom does have many benefits, there are clear drawbacks as well. Limited access to sufficient quantities of a technology, lack of training, the extra time required for the implementations of technology, and the apprehension associated with assessing the effectiveness of technology in the classroom are just a few of the reasons that technology is often not used extensively in the classroom. To understand educational technology one must also understand theories in human behaviour as behaviour is affected by technology.

Media Psychology is the study of media, technology and how and why individuals, groups and societies behave the way they do. The first Ph.D programme with a concentration in media psychology was started in 2002 at Fielding Graduate University by Bernard Luskin. The Media Psychology division of APA, division 46 has a focus on media psychology. Media and the family is another emerging area affected by rapidly changing educational technology.

Digital Divide

One of the greatest barriers of integrating technology into the school system deals with the digital divide. The concept of the digital divide was originally defined as a gap between those who have access to digital technologies and those who do not. This access is associated with age, gender, education, income, ethnicity, and geography. The first deals with the onset of integrating technology into the curriculum and the gap between the digital haves and have nots. In most cases, this form of the digital divide means that those who have access to a computer and the Internet are considered a digital have, while on the other hand, those who do not are considered a digital have not.

In today's society, this is still a significant barrier to implementing technology into the curriculum because the socio-economic status of a school, and its students, will impact whether resources can be purchased and implemented in the school system. Schools that are able to provide technology within the classroom are able to expose their students to a new means of learning, while the students in lower socio-economic schools may miss out on these experiences.

As more and more people have gone online and started using the Internet for an increasing number of activities, researchers have begun to reconsider the notion of the digital divide. Some scholars offered a redefined understanding by seeing the digital divide as a complex and dynamic phenomenon that is essentially multifaced and includes technical access (the physical availability of technology) and social access (the mix of professional knowledge, economic resources, and technical skills required for effectual use of technology).

This means that even if schools and students have access to technology, the ways in which teachers use and introduce it is significant to consider. This form of the digital divide is yet another barrier because it also goes hand-in-hand with the resources the schools have and the training teachers receive. If a teacher, for example, is not well equipped and confident in utilising a form of technology, those students will miss out on gaining the valuable skills required for today's society.

Another factor that plays into the digital divide, which makes it difficult to implement technology into the curriculum, is the generational digital divide. Herrington recognises that the generational divide is interpreted to mean that people on one side of the gap, including the youth, have more access and a greater ability to use new technologies than those on the other side like the adults who were born before the advent of the Internet. The generational digital divide is a common barrier because it challenges teachers to keep up with the ever-changing technology in the classroom.

Even extending beyond the classroom, by the time an individual "adopts a technology, a new one is developed, marketed, and requires a new adoption cycle". Students, who have grown up in a digital environment, may be well acquainted with the on-going process of new technological innovation but may be lacking the guidance they need in order to utilise these technologies effectively. From the teacher's perspective, this process could be an intimidating experience because something as foreign as the computer and Internet must first be learned and then taught to the students in a classroom setting. It is difficult to formulate a curriculum, which aims to integrate technology into the classroom, when the decision-makers are still in the process of learning about it themselves.

Teacher Training

Similar to learning a new task or trade, special training is vital to ensuring the effective integration of classroom technology. The current school curriculum tends to guide teachers in training students to be autonomous problem solvers. This has become a significant barrier to effective training because the traditional methods of teaching have clashed with what is expected in the present workplace. Today's students in the workplace are increasingly being asked to work in teams, drawing on different sets of expertise, and collaborating to solve problem.

These experiences are not highly centered on in the traditional classroom, but are twenty-first century skills that can be attained through the incorporation and engagement with technology. Changes in instruction and use of technology can also promote a higher level of learning among students with different types of intelligence. Therefore since technology is not the end goal of education, but rather a means by which it can be accomplished, educators must have a good grasp of the technology being used and its advantages over more traditional methods. If there is a lack in either of these areas, technology will be seen as a hindrance and not a benefit to the goals of teaching.

Another major issue arises because of the evolving nature of technology. Teachers may find themselves acting as perpetual novices when it comes to learning about technology. This is because technology, including the Internet and its range of applications, is always in a state of change and teachers must attempt to keep current. The ways in which teachers are taught to use technology is also outdated because the primary focus of training is on computer literacy, rather than the deeper, more essential understanding and mastery of technology for information processing, communication, and problem solving.

New resources have to be designed and distributed whenever the technological platform has been changed. However, finding quality materials to support classroom objectives after such changes is often difficult even after they exist in sufficient quantity and teachers must design these resources on their own. The study by Harris notes that the use of random Professional Development days is not adequate enough in order to foster the much-needed skills required to teach and apply technology in the classroom. Learning, therefore, becomes and on-going process, which takes time and a strong commitment among the community of educators. Teacher training faces another drawback when it comes to one's mindset on the integration of technology into the curriculum. The generational divide might also lead to a generational bias, whereby teachers do not feel the need to change the traditional education system because it has been successful in the past. This does not necessarily mean it is the right way to teach for the current and future generations. Considering the fact that today's students are constantly exposed to the impacts of the digital era, learning styles, and the methods of collecting information has evolved. To illustrate this concept Jenkins states, "students often feel locked out of the worlds described in their textbooks through the depersonalised and abstract prose used to describe them," whereas games can construct worlds for players to move through and have some stake in the events unfolding. Even though technology can provide a more personalised, yet collaborative, and creative, yet informative, approach to learning, it may be difficult to motivate the use of these contemporary approaches among teachers who have been in the field for a number of years.

Assessment

Research has shown that there is a great deal of apprehension associated with assessing the effectiveness of technology in the classroom and its development of information-age skills. This is because information-age skills, also commonly referred to as twenty-first century literacies, are relatively new to the field of education. These include "the set of abilities and skills where aural, visual, and digital literacy overlap".

Jenkins modifies this definition by acknowledging them as building on the foundation of traditional literacy, research skills, technical skills and critical-analysis skills taught in the classroom.

Current school assessments are based on standardised tests and the ability to complete these uniform tests, regardless of one's preferred learning style.

Many factors play into this observation including the strong impact of time. By using technology and learning through discovery, teachers may feel that they are not able to cover the material needed to meet the requirements of the curriculum.

Therefore, the traditional style of teaching, including the lecturing in front of the class, and a "one-size-fits-all" approach to testing is common in today's classrooms.

This is a barrier because it prevents the full integration of technology into the curriculum, the ability to learn through enquiry, and the collaborative problem-solving skills, which prove to be essential traits needed in the twenty-first century.

BENEFITS OF EDUCATIONAL TECHNOLOGY

Educational technology is intended to improve education over what it would be without technology.

Some of the claimed benefits are listed below:

- *Easy-to-access course materials:* Instructors can post the course material or important information on a course web site, which means students can study at a time and location they prefer and can obtain the study material very quickly
- *Student motivation:* Computer-based instruction can give instant feedback to students and explain correct answers. Moreover, a computer is patient and non-judgemental, which can give the student motivation to continue learning.

Who studies the effectiveness of computers used for instruction, students usually learn more in less time when receiving computer-based instruction and they like classes more and develop more positive attitudes towards computers in computer-based classes. The American educator, Cassandra B. Whyte, researched and reported about the importance of locus of control and successful academic performance and by the late 1980s, she wrote of how important computer usage and information technology would become in the higher education experience of the future.

- *Wide participation:* Learning material can be used for long distance learning and are accessible to a wider audience
- *Improved student writing:* It is convenient for students to edit their written work on word processors, which can, in turn, improve the quality of their writing. The students are better at critiquing and editing written work that is exchanged over a computer network with students they know
- *Subjects made easier to learn:* Many different types of educational software are designed and developed to help children or teenagers to learn specific subjects. Examples include pre-school software, computer simulators, and graphics software
- *A structure that is more amenable to measurement and improvement of outcomes:* With proper structuring it can become easier to monitor and maintain student work while also quickly gauging modifications to the instruction necessary to enhance student learning.
- *Differentiated Instruction*: Educational technology provides the means to focus on active student participation and to present differentiated questioning strategies. It broadens individualised instruction and promotes the development of personalised learning plans. Students are encouraged to use multimedia components and to incorporate the knowledge they gained in creative ways.

STUDENT SUPPORT SERVICES IN ONLINE DISTANCE EDUCATION

Aoki and Pogroszewski (1998) have presented a model, *The Virtual University Reference Model:*

"Planning and designing a virtual university or a virtual campus is a complex task involving many different aspects of higher education administration and instructional delivery. In the early days of online courses, just putting course syllabi on the Web is worthy of attracting some attention. Nowadays many online courses are offered using a combination of asynchronous and synchronous computer conferencing, slide presentation on the Web, and file transfer systems. Though course delivery is an important component of virtual university, it is not the only component. In order to create a successful academic environment for a distance learner, various support services to students and faculty members have to be included in the plan as integral part of a virtual university." (Ibid.)

The outer ring illustrates how the virtual university is broken down to four major components: administrative services, student services, resource services, and faculty services.

Each component has a different purpose and provides students with different services to support the student's learning. As described by Aoki and Pogroszewski (Ibid.) the second outer ring in the model shows the types of services a student receives from each of the four component areas.

The inner three rings represent (from the innermost): 1) the student and his or her relationship to each of these four areas; 2) transmission systems with which the services can be accessed by students; and 3) applications and tools to be used in offering the service elements in the outer ring.

The students are placed in the centre of the model to point out the importance that all the service components and elements are depicted in relation to the students.

NKI Online Distance Education

NKI was probably the first European online college, and it has offered distance education online every day since 1987. Few - if any - online colleges in the world has been longer in continuous operation.

NKI Distance Education has today well above 300 courses and more than 60 complete study programmes on the Internet. March 2003 we had 4,700 registered active students. Contrary to many other educational providers, where the Internet is used as a supplement to face-to-face teaching or other forms of distance education, we have followed the philosophy that in principle all communication can be taken care of through the Internet, and ideally no obligatory physical meetings should be required. (This does not mean that the students are not free to communicate by post, phone or fax or that study materials includes print, audio or video technologies.)

NKI Internet College '4 Generations' of Development

The NKI Internet College has been developed through 4 systems generations:

1987 - 1994: *'1st generation'* based on the conferencing system 'EKKO', a menu based conferencing system designed by our in-house systems developers no other options were available that could be installed on the mini computer in NKI at that time.

The idea was that we through *'electronic means'* could establish a virtual school and be able to simulate electronically all communication needs previously organised through solutions of combined distance teaching and local face-to-face classes.

1994 - 1995: *'2nd generation'* – *'the open electronic college'* with the underlying philosophy of offering a system as *'open as possible to other networks and services based on the Internet, e-mail and Listserv conferencing* system'.

1996 - 2001: *'3rd generation'* – the introduction of graphical interface and the WWW, taking the step from *'small scale experiments to large scale Internet based distance education'*, introducing courses and programmes below university and college level.

In our experience, it is the step from small-scale to large-scale operation that involves the greatest challenges. Putting some teaching material on the Internet and offer one single course is not a very difficult task. The great challenge is to develop and administer an Internet based teaching organisation offering a large number of courses with high quality to a large number of participants on a continuous basis. This is why we experienced a great leap forward when we March 2001 launched what we characterize as the *'4th generation'* with the introduction of *SESAM (Scalable Educational System for Administration and Management).*

SESAM is our internally developed learning management system completely integrating the teaching-learning system on the WWW with our overall student administrative system (STAS). The learning management system and the student administrative system together form the basis for the complete system of student support services.

Based on theory and research from the field of distance education, included our own research, NKI has chosen this basic philosophy for the development of Internet based education at NKI: *Flexible and individual distance teaching with the student group as social and academic support for learning.* NKI recruits thousands of online students every year.

These students may enrol in any of the more than 60 study programmes or 300 courses or in any combination of courses at any day of the year and progress at their own pace. This flexibility does not exclude group-based solutions in cooperation with one single employer, trade organisation or local organiser.

IMPACT ON INSTRUCTIONAL TECHNOLOGISTS

As part of the federal Individuals with Disabilities Act IDEA amendments of 1997 and 1999, statements now require assistive technology devices and services to be considered on an individualized basis and become a part of the individual education plan (IEP) if the child needs them to benefit from his educational program. The individualized education program (IEP) is a written statement for a child with a disability that is developed, reviewed, and revised at the child's school. The IEPs occur each year for every child with a disability and they are developed by members of the IEP team including parents, teachers, special education teachers, administration and others. Section 508 of the Rehabilitation Act Amendments of 1998 is the most extensive new law with wide ranging effects. This ruling requires that all US federal agencies make their information technology accessible to their employees and customers with disabilities. The law gives federal employees and members of the public the right to sue if the government agency does not provide comparable access to the information and data available to people without disabilities. Section 508 applies to Web sites that are produced for government agencies. All state agencies that receive federal funds under the Assistive Technology Act of 1998 are also required to comply with Section 508 requirements. Schools seeking to comply with legal requirements regarding students with disabilities need faculty with knowledge of assistive technology applications. Based on NCATE accreditation requirements, it would be reasonable for a school administrator or other official to expect that an educational or instructional technology graduate from an NCATE accredited program would be able to effectively contribute to a student's IEP team. These expectations would include that such a graduate be able to make effective judgments and recommendations concerning assistive technology and universal access.

Assistive Technology Course Development

With the rapidly aging population of the United States, there is also a growing need for assistive technology and universal design. To receive federal funding organizations must be IDEA and Section 508 compliant. There exists a need to provide instruction on assistive technologies and methodology to make technology products such as computer programs and web pages handicapped accessible. Instructional and educational technology specialists require more extensive experience and education concerning assistive technology than they currently receive. Instructional/Educational Technology graduate programs should devote a course to the presentation of the basic concepts and applications of assistive technology. This course could be offered as a requirement in the current university master's instructional technology program and as an elective in its master's of education or exceptional education programs. The NCATE and ISTE standards state that for initial certification, a teacher should "demonstrate awareness of resources for adaptive assistive devices for students with special needs." These standards would be well met by such a course. The technologies and strategies presented in a course concerning the application of assistive technology would also address many of the other NCATE guidelines associated with speciality programs such as educational computing and technology leadership.

An assistive technology course could be designed as an introductory or survey course in the application of technology as assistive and adaptive devices, software and strategies. This course could present strategies for students who are physically or mentally impaired, and may be in a mainstreamed situation. The purpose of the course material would be to teach about the use of technologies to overcome handicaps and improve functionality. Course topics could include: basics of assistive technology; legal/ethical issues associated with assistive technology; assistive technology and the individual education plan (IEP); levels of assistive technology; technology adaptations; Windows and Macintosh built-in accessibility tools; text-to-speech and speech-to-text; universal design and the internet; English as a second language, and physical and learning disabilities. An additional facet of such a course should also be designing web-based information to be universally accessible, covering such topics as making web pages more accessible and designing multimedia to overcome user handicaps.

The assessments and activities of the course should include hands-on experiences with assistive technologies. Activities should be designed to include visitations to schools or labs to see assistive technology being used, the application and use of text-to-speech and speech-to-text programs, experiences with adaptive switches and toys, and even experimentation with environmental control hardware and software.

During discussions and interviews with inservice teachers, counsellors, physical therapists, parents, and assistive technology organizations, a need for training and education in the area of assistive technologies was identified.

Through continuing discussions, some basic areas of need in assistive technology education were identified. Visitations were conducted at the Assistive Technology Educational Network (ATEN), Florida Diagnostic Learning Resources (FDLRS) and Florida Instructional Materials (FIMSE) labs.

The goal of the visitations was to learn about the state of the art and the programs being offered, and to understand the components of the AT community. Additional research continued through conducting a literature survey in the field, observing at schools and labs, and studying current Exceptional Student Education (ESE) and Instructional Technology (IT) programs offered at universities.

In order to begin to fill the need that was perceived, a course outline was developed and components were taught at daylong hands-on workshops designed to introduce instructional technologists and teachers to assistive technology. From these preliminary discussions with professionals in the assistive technology community, it was found that an assistive technology course would be appreciated and that course delivery through distance learning would be preferred. Many of the potential students expressing interest in such a course were unable to travel to a university. As an educational technology program course, it would have an added benefit as a recertification course for ESE professionals and general education teachers.

After an initial course outline was developed, members of parent support organizations such as the Statewide Advocacy Network on Disabilities (STAND), university professionals in special education, assistive technology state organizations such as Florida Diagnostic and Learning Resources System (FDLRS) and Assistive Technology Education Network (ATEN), future students in exceptional education, and other instructional technology professionals were asked to provide feedback on the course design, goals, topics and assessments. All were extremely pleased with the idea of the material becoming available for instructional technologists, exceptional student education (ESE) and general education educators.

In its current form, the AT course "Technologies for Special Populations" is designed as an introductory course in the application of technology as assistive and adaptive devices in education. The course itself should model effective design practices. For example web pages will be designed for universal access and course materials and multimedia will be developed to be handicapped accessible. Because of its online delivery, the course serves as a model of information presented through an assistive medium.

Course Learning Strategies

The Technologies for Special Populations course stresses hands-on experiences with various assistive technology approaches and devices. One of the main course goals is designing methods for a student to have actual experiences with the technology going beyond readings and looking at images about the technology.

Students are expected to purchase, train, and use voice input systems, install and use an environmental control system, purchase and use a voice repeater, and use speaking software and hardware devices. Student interactions with assistive technologies fall into five areas. Students interact in an online forum, they have field experiences, and they complete technology projects, in addition to using standard materials such as tests and papers.

One of the strategies used in the Technologies for Special Populations course is the forum. Students participate for themselves and also analyze what other students have done and provide feedback to their classmates' thoughts. Forum topics include case studies that students use in experimenting with, suggesting and explaining assistive technologies. Further forum topics encourage students to discuss and evaluate the impact that the assistive technologies have on them while they use various devices and programs such as environmental control, voice input, and text-to-speech.

Students will be required to observe the use of assistive technology as part of their field experiences. Students are asked to observe a student who uses assistive technology devices, or investigate and visit an assistive technology demonstration lab.

Using an assistive technology device checklist and observation form, students would observe assistive technologies being used and then contribute in an online exchange concerning their observations. Additional experiences include assistive hearing, assistive audio, voice control, DVD applications, and environmental control.

PERSPECTIVES AND MEANING OF EDUCATION TECHNOLOGY

Educational technology is most simply and comfortably defined as an array of tools that might prove helpful in advancing student learning. Educational Technology relies on a broad definition of the word "technology". Technology can refer to material objects of use to humanity, such as machines or hardware, but it can also encompass broader themes, including systems, methods of organization, and techniques. Some modern tools include but are not limited to overhead projectors, laptop computers, and calculators. Newer tools such as "smartphones" and games (both online and offline) are beginning to draw serious attention for their learning potential.

Those who employ educational technologies to explore ideas and communicate meaning are learners or teachers.

Consider the *Handbook of Human Performance Technology*. The word technology for the sister fields of Educational and Human Performance Technology means "applied science." In other words, any valid and reliable process or procedure that is derived from basic research using the "scientific method" is considered a "technology."

Educational or Human Performance Technology may be based purely on algorithmic or heuristic processes, but neither necessarily implies physical technology. The word technology, comes from the Greek "Techne" which means craft or art. Another word "technique", with the same origin, also may be used when considering the field Educational technology. So Educational technology may be extended to include the techniques of the educator.

A classic example of an Educational Psychology text is Bloom's 1956 book, *Taxonomy of Educational Objectives*. Bloom's taxonomy is helpful when designing learning activities to keep in mind what is expected of—and what are the learning goals for— learners. However, Bloom's work does not explicitly deal with educational technology *per se* and is more concerned with pedagogical strategies.

According to some, an Educational Technologist is someone who transforms basic educational and psychological research into an evidence-based applied science (or a technology) of learning or instruction. Educational Technologists typically have a graduate degree (Master's, Doctorate, Ph.D., or D.Phil.) in a field related to educational psychology, educational media, experimental psychology, cognitive psychology or, more purely, in the fields of Educational, Instructional or Human Performance Technology or Instructional (Systems) Design. But few of those listed below as theorists would ever use the term "educational technologist" as a term to describe themselves, preferring terms like "educator". The transformation of educational technology from a cottage industry to a profession is discussed by Shurville, Browne, and Whitaker.

History

One comprehensive history of the field is Saettler's *The evolution of American educational technology*. Another worthy title is Larry Cuban's *Oversold and Underused-Computers in the Classroom*.

For several decades, vendors of equipment such as laptop computers and interactive white boards have been claiming that their technologies would transform classrooms and learning in many positive ways, but there has been little evidence provided to substantiate these claims.

To some extent, the history of educational technology has been marked by a succession of innovations that arrive with much fanfare but often fade into the background once fully tested, as Cuban argues in the above title.

Theories and Practices

Three main theoretical schools or philosophical frameworks

have been present in the educational technology literature. These are Behaviourism, Cognitivism and Constructivism. Each of these schools of thought are still present in today's literature but have evolved as the Psychology literature has evolved.

Behaviourism

This theoretical framework was developed in the early 20th century with the animal learning experiments of Ivan Pavlov, Edward Thorndike, Edward C. Tolman, Clark L. Hull, B.F. Skinner and many others. Many psychologists used these theories to describe and experiment with human learning. While still very useful this philosophy of learning has lost favour with many educators.

Skinner's Contributions

B.F. Skinner wrote extensively on improvements of teaching based on his functional analysis of Verbal Behaviour, and wrote "The Technology of Teaching", an attempt to dispel the myths underlying contemporary education, as well as promote his system he called programmed instruction. Ogden Lindsley also developed the Celeration learning system similarly based on behaviour analysis but quite different from Keller's and Skinner's models.

Cognitivism

Cognitive science has changed how educators view learning. Since the very early beginning of the Cognitive Revolution of the 1960s and 1970s, learning theory has undergone a great deal of change. Much of the empirical framework of Behaviourism was retained even though a new paradigm had begun. Cognitive theories look beyond behaviour to explain brain-based learning. Cognitivists consider how human memory works to promote learning. After memory theories like the Atkinson-Shiffrin memory model and Baddeley's Working memory model were established as a theoretical framework in Cognitive Psychology, new cognitive frameworks of learning began to emerge during the 1970s, 80s, and 90s. It is important to note that Computer Science and Information Technology have had a major influence on Cognitive

Science theory. The Cognitive concepts of working memory (formerly known as short term memory) and long term memory have been facilitated by research and technology from the field of Computer Science. Another major influence on the field of Cognitive Science is Noam Chomsky. Today researchers are concentrating on topics like Cognitive load and Information Processing Theory.

Constructivism

Constructivism is a learning theory or educational philosophy that many educators began to consider in the 1990s. One of the primary tenets of this philosophy is that learners construct their own meaning from new information, as they interact with reality or others with different perspectives.

Constructivist learning environments require students to utilize their prior knowledge and experiences to formulate new, related, and/or adaptive concepts in learning. Under this framework the role of the teacher becomes that of a facilitator, providing guidance so that learners can construct their own knowledge. Constructivist educators must make sure that the prior learning experiences are appropriate and related to the concepts being taught. Jonassen (1997) suggests "well-structured" learning environments are useful for novice learners and that "ill-structured" environments are only useful for more advanced learners. Educators utilizing technology when teaching with a constructivist perspective should choose technologies that reinforce prior learning perhaps in a problem-solving environment.

Connectivism

Connectivism is "a learning theory for the digital age," and has been developed by George Siemens and Stephen Downes based on their analysis of the limitations of behaviourism, cognitivism and constructivism to explain the effect technology has had on how we live, how we communicate, and how we learn. Donald G. Perrin, Executive Editor of the International Journal of Instructional Technology and Distance Learning says the theory "combines relevant elements of many learning theories, social structures, and technology to create a powerful theoretical construct for learning in the digital age."

THE ROLE OF COMPUTER SIMULATIONS IN TEACHING-LEARNING PROCESS

Over the last few years, there has been a great expansion in the computer-assisted methods of teaching and learning. The implementation of such methods into our physics course and laboratories has brought about very effective results. The reasons for our choice to incorporate these powerful computation tools into our courses and laboratories include its assistance to our students in acquiring a better strategy for learning physics, as a demonstration and study of physics concepts and phenomena, and to check results measured from experimental work. We have formulated our own methods of using computer simulations to study physics phenomena based on Adobe Flash CS3 software. Our set of computer simulations allows the students to grasp a deeper understanding of physics phenomena.

We present the set of computer simulations and describe the increase in the interest of students using them for a better success in understanding physical concepts. Also, as example we describe the computer simulation elaborated for the study of the thermal activation energy of intrinsic conduction for a semiconductor. By conducting a statistical survey of the number of functioning computer simulations implemented in our course and laboratories, we notice a rise in the participation of students using them. This suggests that we should encourage the production of more computer simulations. We apply a long term focused teaching-learning strategy in order to improve our physics teaching-learning process. This creates the possibility for our courses and laboratories to be carried out at a higher level, as computer simulations have a great effect on the educational process. An interactive education based on computers advances the effectiveness and efficiency of educational processes. Therefore, students are allowed to further their knowledge and feel better prepared for integration into society.

In the recent years, from the educational viewpoint has been admitted that the classical methods of teachinglearning connected with some computer-assisted methods are good solutions for improving the educational process. The implementation of powerful technologies used in computer based learning leads to the increasing and development of this educational method. At international and national levels, considerable efforts have been made for the implementation of adequate software in the educational process. Concerning the continue improvement of our physics course and laboratories, a very important task is to describe various physical phenomena and bring them alive with help of computer simulations.

The technical issue includes computational requirements, modern and powerful software and hardware. We have incorporated these powerful computational tools in the educational process for assisting students to achieve a better understanding of physics concepts and phenomena, and to check the results obtained from experimental work. We have developed a strategy for teaching students how to operate and realise an interactive use of adequate software for exploring, learning and applying physics laws. Our set of computer simulations is elaborated using Adobe Flash CS3 software. For a high level of performance we have optimized continually the applications. We notice a continue improvement of students understanding and an increasing of interest concerning the work at the physics laboratories. Students have become more motivated and this has been the reason for the production of more computer simulations. We provide a study of the role of computer simulations in the computer-assisted educational process. We performed a statistical survey of the number of computer simulations implemented in our course and laboratories through the recent years. This study enlightened a rise in the participation of students that used the computer simulations. Also, for illustrating our work we present the computer application elaborated for the study of the thermal activation energy of intrinsic conduction for a semiconductor.

Implementation of computer simulations in the teaching-learning process

The development of computational technologies has determined an increasing of the implementation of new computational programmes in engineering education. The computer assisted education provides a framework for the integration of new and powerful computational tools and especially of the computer simulations of physics phenomena. Our long-term experience in the field of physics has demonstrated the usefulness of processing data using the computer simulations. We do not intend to make a complete replacement of the traditional methods of teaching and learning physics, but we want to perform a good understanding of physics laws and phenomena.

In this light, we have provided our physics laboratories with a set of computer simulations that allow the students to develop skills of measurement and analysis. Also, the computer simulations are not affected by the errors generated by the measurement process and the sensibility of apparatus, and can be used as checking tools for the laboratory work. for the results obtained from experimental work We have created a set of interactive physics simulations using computer applications to illustrate some key phenomena and laws of physics concerning oscillations, waves, thermodynamics and optical phenomena. These computer simulations are used in our physics laboratory since 2006 and most of them are elaborated in Adobe Flash CS3. We own a suite of twelve different simulations of our laboratory works regarding various physics phenomena, detailing many aspects of physics studied in the course that we offer. It was very important to decide which physics laboratories need computer simulation activities, and amongst these, which hold more priority.

We have collaborated with our students in order to establish which laboratory works are more suitable for computer simulations, taking in account their arguments and options. After sorting the experiments into the order of priority, we have elaborated the computer simulations so that they have to yield the same results as those of experimental results. A comparison between the practical experiment and the simulation can be made by the students, as the software is able to run during or after the experiment. We chose the animation and programming environment of Adobe Flash CS3 for the elaboration of simulations motivated by its flexibility and advanced graphical facilities. Many applications, animations and web pages are created and processed in this professional software. The operations, the functions and the user friendly style allow users who are developing Flash applications access to extraordinary possibilities.

This differentiates Flash as a robust and exciting environment for developing applications. The applications use data that has been collected from physical experiments in order to allow the simulation to describe the behaviour and indications of the laboratory equipment as accurately as possible. Necessary physical formulas are applied to obtain the results. Using the experimental data acquired from certain sites within a given period of time, an interpolation of 1st degree could be implemented in these applications. As a result, the user can analyse simulation values within the same time span as that of the experiment.

Therefore, the user can choose a value, without being constricted to a limited number of values or even by only the experimental values. We ensure that the applications have a menu in Romanian and English, so that the user may choose just as to preference or necessity. Each application allows the students to verify experimental data, calculate formulas and construct and present graphs. As an example, we present the application elaborated for the determination of the thermal activation energy of intrinsic conduction for a semiconductor. We present the screen-shots of the applications interface. The computer interface image for the lab objectives, the apparatus and equipment, and the measurements and procedure. The aim of the computer simulation is the determination of the thermal activation energy of intrinsic conduction for a semiconductor. For the determination of the thermal activation energy of intrinsic conduction for a semiconductor the dependence between the resistance and temperature of a thermistor is used.

The components of the experimental equipment are:

- A thermistor with the terminals coupled to an electronic ohmmeter;
- An electronic ohmmeter by means of which the resistance is measured;

- Heat source, that is a 40-W bulb;
- Temperature probe, mounted next to the thermistor and connected to it by thermal contact.

The information from the temperature probe is sent to an electronic thermostat programmable in the range 0-100 C equipped with a graded scale. For usual practice, the range 0-60 C is recommended. To open the application, the students have to press the switch on the electronic thermostat and to choose the values of temperature for which the values of resistance will be indicated by the electronic ohmmeter. After they have entered the first value of the temperature, which is indicated to be greater than the temperature of surroundings, they have to increase the values of the temperature and to read the corresponding values of the resistance.

Otherwise, a warning indicated by a yellow box flashing next to the value of temperature which corresponds to the equilibrium state of the value of the resistance has to be read. After the values that observe the possible value ranges are entered, the button Upgrade will be pressed as it displays the obtained values of $10^3/T$, R and lnR, upgrading at the same time the graphic which gives the dependence between lnR and $10^3/T$. The computer interface image for the laboratory objectives, measurements and procedure and the components of the experimental equipment. This screenshot allows the students to become familiar with the theory and experimental method.

Discussion

In the last decade, more students and physicists are involved in the use of computer simulations for providing a better understanding of concepts and physics phenomena. In our work we present a set of 12 computer simulations and point out the increase in the interest of students using these computer applications for a better success in processing the experimental data with aid of efficient and accurate computational tools. Most of our computer simulations for the physics laboratory are elaborated in Adobe Flash CS3 programme. As an illustrative example we describe the computer simulation prepared for the study of the thermal activation energy of intrinsic conduction for a semiconductor. In addition, we give a statistical study of the number of functioning computer simulations implemented in our course and laboratories.

The rise in the participation of students that are interested in computer simulations of physics phenomena make us to produce more computer simulations. Because the process of collecting experimental data is affected by errors we offer to the students the possibility of using virtual tools like computer simulations. The computer simulations are not affected by experimental errors and can be used as checking tools for the results obtained from experimental work. We are confident, and the large participation of our students support this, that computer simulations have improved the teaching-learning process. Further, the computer simulations allow students to become more familiar with the virtual labs and a comparative mode of learning, and how to experiment and use software applications. In the future, we want to implement the set of physics simulations in the distance learning via the Internet (e-learning). Applying an interactive education based on the use of computers simulations we improve our courses and laboratories, which are carried out at a higher level, and we advance the effectiveness and efficiency of educational processes. Therefore, students are allowed to further their knowledge and feel better prepared for integration into society.

THE NATURE OF TECHNOLOGY IN LEARNING

Throughout the 20th century there were developments of the role of technology in learning. Pressey's testing machine of 1926-27 is well known but his main contribution to educational technology lay not so much in his machine as in his strong belief that an industrial revolution in education was about to dawn, bringing great benefits of more effective and more efficient learning. He pursued this dream for several decades, although he had little time for programmed learning or for teaching machines when these came along. Even his own machines were thrown away in favour of a small card with blobs of ink on it; the learner erased the blob over the answer he thought correct, and underneath was a symbol that told him whether he was right. "We are on the threshold of an exciting and revolutionary period, in which the scientific study of man will be put to work in man's best interest. Education must play its part. It must accept that a sweeping revision of educational practices is possible and inevitable". With such evalgelising zeal did Skinner write in his 1954 article The Science of Learning and the Art of Teaching.

Skinner saw four serious shortcomings in the educational system:

- The reinforcers used were still aversive
- They were used too long after responses had been elicited
- The progression towards the required behaviour was poorly arranged
- Reinforcement was provided too infrequently.

Skinner suggested that few teachers, if any, could remedy these shortcomings working alone with a group of pupils and proposed that machines might be employed to perform most of the function the teacher could not perform, as well as some of those she could. Skinner saw programmed learning and teaching machines as part (if not all) of an overall improvement in teaching techniques. The use of technology in learning is different in its use in traditional group-based face-to-face teaching and in distance education, which is frequently individual-based and separates the learner not only from the teacher but also from the learning group.

Traditional group-based face-to-face education and training has used technology as a supplement to the teacher, and differs from distance education in which technology is a substitute for the teacher. However, in the late 1990s, with the arrival of the WWW and the provision of some universities of web based courses in place of lectures, the web has become an option on the campus as well as at a distance.

In distance education one can follow the development of a series of developments of the use of technology for teaching. The first generation uses the technology of printing and was basically the provision of print based materials for learning. A second generation added multimedia including audio, video and CD

Roms to replace or supplement the print-based materials. The third generation of the 1990s was the impact of eLearning and the arrival of the WWW.

E-SOURCES FOR LEARNING, CD-ROM

CD-ROM is a pre-pressed compact disc that contains data accessible to, but not writable by, a computer. While the compact disc format was originally designed for music storage and playback, the 1985 "Yellow Book" standard developed by Sony and Philips adapted the format to hold any form of binary data.

Five years later CD-ROM drives were being introduced on to computers. In 1994, they called a computer with a CD-ROM a Multimedia computer since it could play music and specially coded videos. Companies like Creative Technologies created a Sound Blaster multimedia upgrade kit which at the time gave the user a CD-ROM Drive with driver, a sound card and speakers. This in 1994 was a $200 product. Windows 95 in 1995 was introduced on either 10, 3.5-inch disks or 1 CD-ROM.

CD-ROMs are popularly used to distribute computer software, including games and multimedia applications, though any data can be stored (up to the capacity limit of a disc). Some CDs hold both computer data and audio with the latter capable of being played on a CD player, while data (such as software or digital video) is only usable on a computer (such as PC CD-ROMs). These are called enhanced CDs.

Although many people use lowercase letters in this acronym, proper presentation is in all capital letters with a hyphen between CD and ROM. It was also suggested by some, especially soon after the technology was first released, that CD-ROM was an acronym for "Compact Disc read-only-*media*", or that it was a more "correct" definition. This was not the intention of the original team who developed the CD-ROM, and common acceptance of the "memory" definition is now almost universal. This is probably in no small part due to the widespread use of other "ROM" acronyms such as Flash-ROMs and EEPROMs where "memory" is usually the correct term.

Media

CD-ROM discs are identical in appearance to audio CDs, and data are stored and retrieved in a very similar manner (only differing from audio CDs in the standards used to store the data). Discs are made from a 1.2 mm thick disc of polycarbonate plastic, with a thin layer of aluminium to make a reflective surface. The most common size of CD-ROM disc is 120 mm in diameter, though the smaller Mini CD standard with an 80 mm diameter, as well as numerous non-standard sizes and shapes (e.g. business card-sized media) are also available. Data is stored on the disc as a series of microscopic indentations. A laser is shone onto the reflective surface of the disc to read the pattern of pits and lands ("pits", with the gaps between them referred to as "lands"). Because the depth of the pits is approximately one-quarter to one-sixth of the wavelength of the laser light used to read the disc, the reflected beam's phase is shifted in relation to the incoming beam, causing destructive interference and reducing the reflected beam's intensity. This pattern of changing intensity of the reflected beam is converted into binary data.

Standard

There are several formats used for data stored on compact discs, known collectively as the Rainbow Books. These include the original Red Book standards for CD audio, White Book and Yellow Book CD-ROM. The ECMA-130 standard, which gives a thorough description of the physics and physical layer of the CD-ROM, inclusive of Cross-interleaved Reed-Solomon coding (CIRC) and Eight-to-Fourteen Modulation, can be downloaded from.

ISO 9660 defines the standard file system of a CD-ROM, although it is due to be replaced by ISO 13490. UDF format is used on user-writeable CD-R and CD-RW discs that are intended to be extended or overwritten. The bootable CD specification, to make a CD emulate a hard disk or floppy, is called El Torito. Apparently named this because its design originated in an El Torito restaurant in Irvine, California.

CD-ROM drives are rated with a speed factor relative to music CDs (1x or 1-speed which gives a data transfer rate of 150 kilobytes per second). 12x drives were common in April 1997. Above 12x speed, there are problems with vibration and heat. Constant angular velocity (CAV) drives give speeds up to 20x but due to the nature of CAV the actual throughput increase over 12x is less than 20/12.

CD-ROM format

A CD-ROM *sector* contains 2352 bytes, divided into 98 24-byte frames. Unlike a music CD, a CD-ROM cannot rely on error concealment by interpolation, and therefore requires a higher reliability of the retrieved data. In order to achieve improved error correction and detection, a CD-ROM has a third layer of Reed-Solomon error correction. A Mode-1 CD-ROM, which has the full three layers of error correction data, contains a net 2048 bytes of the available 2352 per sector. In a Mode-2 CD-ROM, which is mostly used for video files, there are 2336 user-available bytes per sector. The net byte rate of a Mode-1 CD-ROM, based on comparison to CDDA audio standards, is 44.1k/s×4B×2048/2352 = 153.6 kB/s. The playing time is 74 minutes, or 4440 seconds, so that the net capacity of a Mode-1 CD-ROM is 682 MB or, equivalently, 650 MiB.

A 1x speed CD drive reads 75 consecutive sectors per second.

CD sector contents

- A standard 74 min CD contains 333,000 blocks or sectors.
- Each sector is 2352 bytes, and contains 2048 bytes of PC (MODE1) Data, 2336 bytes of PSX/VCD (MODE2) Data, or 2352 bytes of AUDIO.
- The difference between sector size and data content are the Headers info and the Error Correction Codes, that are big for Data (high precision required), small for VCD (standard for video) and none for audio.
- If extracting the disc in RAW format (standard for creating images) always extract 2352 bytes per sector, not 2048/2336/2352 bytes depending on data type (basically, extracting the whole sector). This fact has two main consequences:

  - Recording data CDs at very high speed (40x) can be done without losing information. However, as audio CDs do not contain a third layer of error correction codes, recording these at high speed may result in more unrecoverable errors or 'clicks' in the audio.
  - On a 74 minute CD, one can fit larger images using RAW mode, up to 333,000 × 2352 = 783,216,000 bytes (747~ MB). This is the upper limit for RAW images created on a 74 min or 650~ MB Red Book CD. The 14.8% increase is due to the discarding of error correction data
- Please note that an image size is *always* a multiple of 2352 bytes (the size of a block) when extracting in RAW mode.

Manufacture

Pre-pressed CD-ROMs are mass-produced by a process of stamping where a glass master disc is created and used to make "stampers", which are in turn used to manufacture multiple copies of the final disc with the pits already present. Recordable (CD-R) and rewritable (CD-RW) discs are manufactured by a similar method, but the data are recorded on them by a laser changing the properties of a dye or phase change material in a process that is often referred to as "burning".

Capacity

CD-ROM capacities are normally expressed with binary prefixes, subtracting the space used for error correction data. A standard 120 mm, "700 MB" CD-ROM can hold about 847 MB of data, or 737 MB (703 MiB) with error correction. In comparison, a single-layer DVD-ROM can hold 4.7 GB of error-protected data, more than 6 CD-ROMs.

CD-ROM Drives

CD-ROM discs are read using CD-ROM drives. A CD-ROM drive may be connected to the computer via an IDE (ATA), SCSI, SATA, Firewire, or USB interface or a proprietary interface, such as the Panasonic CD interface. Virtually all modern CD-ROM drives can also play audio CDs as well as Video CDs and other data standards when used in conjunction with the right software.

Laser and Optics

CD-ROM drives employ a near-infrared 780 nm laser diode. The laser beam is directed onto the disc via an opto-electronic tracking module, which then detects whether the beam has been reflected or scattered.

Transfer Rates

The rate at which CD-ROM drives can transfer data from the disc is gauged by a speed factor relative to music CDs: 1x or 1-speed which gives a data transfer rate of 150 kilobytes per second in the most common data format. By increasing the speed at which the disc is spun, data can be transferred at greater rates. For example, a CD-ROM drive that can read at 8x speed spins the disc at up to 4000 rpm (compared to the 500 rpm maximum for 1x speed), giving a transfer rate of 1.2 megabytes per second. Above 12x speed, vibration and heat can become a problem. CD-ROM drives above this speed tackle the problem in several ways. Constant angular velocity (CAV) drives spin the disc at a constant rate, leading to faster data transfer when reading from the outer parts of the disc, but slower towards the centre. 20x was thought to be the maximum speed due to mechanical constraints until Samsung Electronics introduced the SCR-3230, a 32x CD-ROM drive which uses a ball bearing system to balance the spinning disc in the drive to reduce vibration and noise. As of 2004, the fastest transfer rate commonly available is about 52x or 10,350 rpm and 7.62 megabytes per second, though this is only when reading information from the outer parts of a disc. Future speed increases based simply upon spinning the disc faster are particularly limited by the strength of polycarbonate plastic used in CD manufacturing, since at 52x, the linear velocity of the outermost part of the disk is around 65 meters per second (234 km/h or 146.3mph (0.12m x pi x 10350rpm / 60 = 65m/s)) which presents a danger of injury should the disk disintegrate due to the lack of sufficient centripetal force in the disc at these speeds. (Indeed, severe damage to computer hardware was the consistent result as CD manufacturers tested the limits of the polycarbonate in controlled environments.) However, improvements can still be obtained by the use of multiple laser pickups as demonstrated by the Kenwood True-X 72x which uses seven laser beams and a rotation speed of approximately 10x.

CD-Recordable drives are often sold with three different speed ratings, one speed for write-once operations, one for re-write operations, and one for read-only operations. The speeds are typically listed in that order; ie a 12x/10x/32x CD drive can, CPU and media permitting, write to CD-R discs at 12x speed (1.80 MB/s), write to CD-RW discs at 10x speed (1.50 MB/s), and read from CD discs at 32x speed (4.80 MB/s).

The 1x speed rating for CD-ROM (150 kB/s) is different than 1x speed rating for audio CD (172.3 kB/s) and is not to be confused with the 1x speed rating for DVDs (1.32 MB/s).

Copyright Issues

There has been a move by the recording industry to make audio CDs (CDDAs, Red Book CDs) unplayable on computer CD-ROM drives, to prevent the copying of music. This is done by intentionally introducing errors onto the disc that the embedded circuits on most stand-alone audio players can automatically compensate for, but which may confuse CD-ROM drives. Consumer rights advocates are as of October 2001 pushing to require warning labels on compact discs that do not conform to the official Compact Disc Digital Audio standard (often called the Red Book) to inform consumers of which discs do not permit full fair use of their content.

In 2005, Sony BMG Music Entertainment was criticised when a copy protection mechanism known as Extended Copy Protection (XCP) used on some of their audio CDs automatically and surreptitiously installed copy-prevention software on computers. Such discs are not legally allowed to be called CDs or Compact Discs because they break the Red Book standard governing CDs, and Amazon.com for example describes them as "copy protected discs" rather than "compact discs" or "CDs".

Software distributors, and in particular distributors of computer games, often make use of various copy protection schemes to prevent software running from any media besides the original CD-ROMs. This differs somewhat from audio CD protection in that it is usually implemented in both the media and the software itself. The CD-ROM itself may contain "weak" sectors to make copying the disc more difficult, and additional data that may be difficult or impossible to copy to a CD-R or disc image, but which the software checks for each time it is run to ensure an original disc and not an unauthorized copy is present in the computer's CD-ROM drive.

Manufacturers of CD writers (CD-R or CD-RW) are encouraged by the music industry to ensure that every drive they produce has a unique identifier, which will be encoded by the drive on every disc that it records: the RID or Recorder Identification Code. This is a counterpart to the SID—the Source Identification Code, an eight character code beginning with "IFPI" that is usually stamped on discs produced by CD recording plants.

5

Strategy of Online Teaching in Modern Era

The literature regarding best practices in online teaching strategies can be organized into three major components of the instructional process:

- Planning and development,
- Teaching in action, and
- Student assessment and data evaluation.

Together, these three components significantly influence the effectiveness of the online environment, making it especially important that instructors are aware of best practice teaching strategies.

Best Practices in Planning and Development

One of the most important elements of planning and managing online courses is instructors' recognition of the fact that although there are a wide array of educational technologies and course management tools available for online teaching, not all of these technologies are appropriate matches to the subject taught and the teacher's pedagogical style and strategies. As such, it is very important that instructors ensure that pedagogical principles drive the use of technology rather than the other way around. Instructors must strive to achieve certain learning standards, regardless of the medium through which they are teaching. Because of this, course planning should take place before instructors select the technology and course management system that will be used for the course.

The first step in the planning process involves the development of learning objectives. The importance of learning objective development and communication is highlighted throughout the literature, including Park University's guidelines for the creation of learning objectives:

- *Behaviour*: Learning objectives should be written in terms of observable behavioural outcomes. Clear, targeted verbs should be used to communicate with students the expected outcomes of learning activities.
- *Student-Centred*: All learning objectives should focus on the student. Effective objectives explain expectation for student behaviour, performance, and understanding.
- *Conditions*: Learning objectives should be specific and should target one aspect of understanding. The conditions of the objective include the tools, references, and/or aids that will be provided to the student.
- *Standards*: Each learning objective should be measurable and should include the criteria for student assessment. Standards are important because they both inform students of performance expecta-tions while providing insight as to how these expectations will be measured.

Following the development of clearly defined learning objectives and the special needs of students, instructors may begin to select the technological option best-suited for the course. It is important to note, however, that although there is tremendous variety in the educational technologies available to online instructors, the field of distance learning technology is changing quickly, and it is therefore necessary for instructors and administrators to keep a close eye on emerging trends and associated best practices.

For example, the annual Horizon Report, a long-running qualitative research project that seeks to identify and describe emerging education technologies, projects that mobile technologies, cloud computing, geocoded data, personal web programmes, semantic-aware applications, and smart objects will significantly impact the choices of educational institutions within the next five years.

While these six technologies in online education are still emerging as educational tools, online technologies such as web-pages, discussion forums, course management systems, audio tools, and video tools are well-entrenched in the field of online instruction. However, with each technology comes a number of planning considerations that are important for online instructors to reflect upon as they develop their courses and choose the most appropriate technologies. The University of Washington's "Learning and Scholarly Technologies," a website that provides a help centre for online instructors, addresses a number of these technological considerations.

One final yet very important factor that should be taken into consideration in the planning and development component of online teaching strategy is the need for the online courses to be delivered in such a way as to create a learning community among students and the instructor. Research shows that many of the instances in which distance education courses fail to promote student learning, the cause is students' sense of isolation or low level of self-directedness.

In order to combat this isolation factor, successful online courses develop established protocols for building, maintaining, and evaluating student-to-student and student-to-faculty interactions. Teaching methods including training in technology for distance learning students, interactive teaching that fosters critical dialogue, mentoring, cooperative peer learning, group out-of-class activities, and the use of e-mail or web announcements to inform students about opportunities for interaction should be designed into the online course to enhance student learning.

Practices in Teaching-in-Action

As discussed earlier in this report, the level of interaction among students and between students and the instructor is particularly important in online instruction. Distance education provides many opportunities to foster an interactive "classroom," including two of the most commonly used pedagogical techniques to promote interactivity:

- Online discussion forums and
- Student collaboration on assignments.

Online discussion forums are one of the best ways to facilitate interaction and learning in the online classroom, in part due to their ability to promote constructivist thinking, critical thinking, and higher-order thinking, all while distributing knowledge among all the students in the class. Additionally, discussion is a relatively simple way to encourage interaction in the online environment. For example, interactive learning can be promoted through the use of e-mail or electronic discussion tools, such as the University of Washington's Catalyst GoPost tool, a web-based discussion board where students can compare notes, discuss assignments, post attachments, or work together, and the Google platform, Wiki, a tool which allows individuals to create websites which can be viewed and edited by site members.

However, regardless of the technologies used, online discussion forums lose effectiveness without the development of thoughtful and relevant questions and instructor's moderation of responses.

The following guidelines are recommended to promote the important element, constructivist thinking, in the online discussion and pedagogy:

- Pose a stimulating question,
- Brainstorm answers to the question,
- Compare ideas, and
- Fuse to the curriculum.

The first step in this process, "Pose a stimulating question," deserves special focus due to its important role in determining the direction of online discussion. As such, it is recommended that instructors consider the cognitive levels of the questions, the educational situation, the goals and objectives of the instruction, and the needs of the students when designing online discussion questions. A survey of the types of discussion questions used by online instructors revealed that the questions could be grouped into the following categories:

- *Interest-getting and attention-getting questions:*
  - *Example*: "If you awakened in the year 2399, what is the first thing you would notice?"
- *Diagnosing and checking questions*:
  - Example: "Does anyone know Senge's five principles of a learning organization?"
- *Recall of specific facts or information questions*:
  - *Example*: "Who can name the main characters in Moby Dick?"
- *Managerial questions*:
  - *Example*: "Did you request an extension on the assignment due date?
- *Structure and redirect learning questions*:
  - *Example*: "Now that we have discussed the advantages of, and limitations to, formative evaluation, who can do the same for summative evaluation?"
- *Allow expression of affect questions*:
  - *Example*: "How did you feel about our online guest's list of ten things trainers do to shoot themselves in the foot?"
- *Encourage higher level thought processes questions*:
  - Example: "Considering what you have read, and what was discussed in the posts this past week, can you summarize all the ways there are to overcome obstacles to effective teamwork?"

During the discussion process, it is important that instructors continuously manage students' ideas and further facilitate interactions. However, if the online discussion is going well without instructor feedback, it is often best for teachers to wait to jump into the discussion until the students' responses are waning. At that point, it is recommended that instructors summarize key points or ask prompting questions to recharge the discussion. The second strategy to facilitate interactivity: "encourage student collaboration," relies on the use of educational technologies to simulate face-to-face meetings when students work together on assignments. However, it should be noted that a review of the literature identified one study that found that while instructors perceive the learner-instructor and learner-learner interactions as key factors in quality online instruction, students' varied regarding their opinion on whether interaction is important.

The authors of the study suggest that this variance in student opinion is related to differences in learning style and personality, as well as students' lowered expectations of the quality of interaction in online instruction. While these findings emphasize that instructors need to identify the needs of their students in online instruction, they also suggest that interaction is considered by both teachers and students to influence the effectiveness of instruction in a primarily positive way. Beyond these two major pedagogical strategies for enhancing the success of online teaching, Pennsylvania State University's World Camus, which offers more than 50 degree and certificate programmes through distance and online education, provides a detailed guide of best practices strategies and pedagogical advice for online teaching.

This is a set of best practice recommendations and related strategies for the process of teaching, the majority of which directly compliment the literature asserting the need for interactivity, instructor presence, student collaboration, and the creation of a learning community.

Prepare Your Students for Learning Online

Online instructors need to provide sufficient orientation for students regarding the technology and instructional methods used in the course.

This can be accomplished by:

- Posting a welcome message to help students get started.
- Include a brief orientation for students to get familiar with the terminology and tools used in the course management system.
- Provide contact information for technical help in a variety of places, as well as personal contact information, standard response times, and preferred communication methods.
- Remind students to set up e-mail forwarding to their preferred accounts. However, faculty and students should

keep all course-related communications within the course management system to maintain confidentiality.

- Provide online office hours as needed.
- Structure the course by providing guidelines for participation and other policies to help students learn more effectively.
- Provide resources and strategies for online learning and explain how online learning is different from classroom learning.
- Include a Student FAQ with common questions about courses, registration, tuition, financial aid, course materials and software.

Specify Course Goals, Expectations, and Policies

It is important to provide course goals, expectations, structure, and related course/departmental/institutional policies at the beginning of the course.

These elements are commonly included in course syllabus, although they may be placed elsewhere.

Important information includes:

- Course goals and learning objectives, including a description of course structure.
- Required and optional course materials or textbooks.
- Clear and specific grading policies and academic integrity policies.
- The guidelines for student participation and collaboration, including any recommendations for online communication, policies for assignment submission and grading, and web etiquette guidelines for online courses.

Build a Learning Community

A variety of literature asserts the need for online instructors to build learning communities that engage students.

Learning communities can be built by:

- Welcoming students before the course begins via e-mail

or course announcement. This welcome should be resent after the add/drop period ends.

- Posting a personal introduction with an informal tone.
- Providing lots of encouragement and support, particularly in the beginning of the course. This includes positive feedback administered to students privately by e-mail.
- Encouraging students to create their own homepage, or post a short self-introduction to the discussion forum. Alternatively students can be encouraged to develop a social space by creating a group inside or outside of the course site.
- Uploading any relevant pictures to the course site, and encouraging students to do so as well.

Promote Active Learning

The online teaching strategy should foster students' active, constructive participation in learning.

This can be accomplished by instructors that:

- Emphasize to students the importance of learning by playing an active role in the learning process, a role which differs from the direct instruction or lecture in traditional classrooms.
- Provide opportunities for students to critique and reflect upon certain course topics.
- Encourage students to use the Internet for researching course topics, but remind them to be critical about the information they find and share.
- Encourage students to be proactive learners by regularly logging into the course site, submitting assignments on-time, participating in discussions, and cooperating with teammates.
- Provide opportunities for active problem solving and for team work.
- Encourage the active participation in online discussion by designing provocative questions, encouraging students to respond to questions at a deeper level, and by pointing out any opposing perspectives.

- Use multiple discussion formats, including small group discussions, "buzz groups", case studies, team debates, "jigsaw groups" where subgroups discuss parts of a topic and then collaborate on their findings, and role play.

Model Effective Online Interaction

- *Instructors can model effective interaction through frequent interactions with students that*:
  - Respond to student comments and questions within time frames set at the beginning of the course. Instructors make sure to notify students if these time frames change, or if they will be unavailable for some period during the semester.
  - Provide general feedback to the entire class on specific assignments or discussions, while at the same time providing individual encouragement and comments to students. Feedback on graded assignments should recognize good work and make suggestions for improvement.
  - Provide a weekly "wrap up" before the next session, and introduce each new week with an overview of the session plan and deadlines.

Encourage Lagging Students

Because students have different learning styles, instructors should monitor students and identify those who are lagging. Important points to aid the monitoring process include:

- Instructors' awareness that students who fall behind are in jeopardy of not completing the course, which may endanger their financial aid.
- Use of available educational technology tools, such as course management systems, to track student progress in course activities.
- Contact students who haven't logged in for over a week to inquire whether they're experiencing technical difficulties or problems with course content/activities. If

students can't participate due to technical problems, connect them immediately to technical help.

- Contact students who have not completed assignments by e-mail or phone.
- Include flexibility in grading if possible

Assess Students' Messages in Online Discussion

Instructors should assess students' messages in online discussion forums through a set a specific criteria. These assessment criteria for online discussion should be included in the course syllabus, a course announcement, or within the instructions for the discussion task.

Criteria should:

- Make sure the assessment criteria measure both the quantity and quality of the online message.
- Consider assigning points to messages that encourage additional posting.
- Make use of recommended rubrics from the literature.

Examples of good rubrics include:

- Edelstein and Edwards' Assessing Effectiveness of Student Participation in Online Discussions. This rubric considers five categories that are important for building a learning community: promptness and initiative, delivery of post, relevance of post, expression within the post, and contribution to the learning community.
- Garrison's, *et al.* Cognitive Processing Categories. *May be useful when assessing the quality of postings*:
  1. Triggering;
  2. Exploration,
  3. Integration, and
  4. Solution.
- Kleinman's Grading Rubric for Online Discussion Participation. Provides detailed grading criteria.

Motivation and Provide Feedback and Support

There are a variety of teaching strategies to support, guide, and motivate students to learn actively in the online environment, including:

- Provide opportunities for student collaboration and facilitate collaborative learning processes and tools such as Breeze.
- Choose a conversational tone that makes students feel comfortable in the online learning environment and that establishes trust in communication while building a learning community.
- Provide meaningful feedback to all assignments and comments.
- Provide a weekly summary of discussion topics to demonstrate your participation, and assess messages for both quantity and quality.

Similarly, it helps to provide feedback and support to students through the:

- Encouragement of students to articulate their confusion or difficulty with course content, projects, requirements, or instructions for activities.
- Quick response to students' concerns or technical difficulties.
- Use of peer assessment to provide additional feedback to students while reducing faculty workload.
- Participation in online discussion by encouraging openness in online discussions, diagnosing misconceptions immediately to avoid confusion, providing additional resources, and encouraging student to use examples, case studies, or literature to support their arguments.

Encourage Students to Regulate Their Own Learning

In order to succeed, students must be encouraged to become "self-regulated learners."

Strategies to accomplish this self-regulation include:

- Allowing students to become "process managers" in the online course by giving up some of the traditional power of teachers. For example, students may be directed to take turns leading online learning experiences.

- Encouraging students' reflection and feedback through the inclusion of an introductory survey with questions on student expectations for the course and engagement in students' course evaluations.
- Allowing students to take responsibility for their peers' learning as well as their own through discussion forums.
- Provide opportunities for peer review.

Understand the Impact of Multiculturalism

It is important that online instructors understand and are aware of cultural-based differences in online classrooms, and that they cultivate cultural sensitivity in e-learning through the appropriate use of technology.

This can be accomplished by:

- Using non-discriminatory language and being aware that cultural diversity exists both in nationality/ethnicity as well as in generation, religion, political beliefs, or socioeconomic status.
- For difficult, emotional, or controversial topics, use chats or threaded discussions, or make discussion optional. At the same time, threaded discussions can be used to invite feedback and reflection on the topic.
- If possible, by creating teams of students from diverse backgrounds to encourage cross-cultural facilitation.
- Providing high-quality resources to explain conflicting perspectives.
- Providing appropriate supports if it is suspected that a culturally related factor may negatively affect an online learning experience.
- Joining professional teaching communities or conferences to gain exposure and connections to our global society.

Deal with Conflicts Promptly

Conflicts should be dealt with promptly to minimize student distractions.

Conflict management strategies include:

- The provision of web etiquette guidelines.
- Intervention only when conflicts intensify to a point where students can no longer work through the issue on their own. Otherwise, conflict should be welcomed as a sign that the learning community is developing.
- Private communication with students who are posting inappropriately, and contacting the appropriate department if you suspect that a student has violated academic integrity policies.
- Provide a regular peer evaluation function so that students can communicate their impressions on how the group is functioning.

Practices in Student Assessment and Data Evaluation

Best practice recommendations for the assessment of student learning in an online environment include:

- Assessment through an evaluation process that uses several methods and applies specific standards for student learning.
- The regular review of intended learning outcomes to ensure clarity, utility, and appropriateness.
- Timely evaluations at regular intervals to increase course flexibility for students.
- The assurance that monitoring/proctoring policies are in place during assessments of student learning.
- The integration of some sort of verification method to ensure academic integrity.
- Assessment strategies are integral to the learning experience, enabling learners to assess their progress, identify areas for review, and re-establish immediate learning or sessions goals.
- Strategies are varied and aligned to instructional goals.
- Assessment criteria are clearly articulated.

Pennsylvania State University's World Campus' guide of best practice online teaching strategies also emphasizes the need for instructors to gather and analysis student evaluation data to improve course content and pedagogy. Student data can be collected and used through many methods, including the use of a discussion board for anonymous course feedback, the encouragement and rewarding of students who report significant errors in course content, and through the review of faculty evaluations to provide feedback for future course redesign.

Finally, best practices in online teaching assert that instructors should be careful to follow intellectual property guidelines, participate in an online teaching community to learn from peers, and learn to manage time effectively. Instructors' ability to manage time and workload effectively is especially important because there are no set hours to online instruction, making it easy for online teachers to become overwhelmed.

In order to manage time effectively, it is suggested that instructors use the following guidelines:

- Set limits,
- Do not always be available to learners,
- Establish clear priorities for dealing with messages,
- Put time limits on discussion,
- Provide learners with predetermined answers to frequently asked questions,
- Encourage learners to find local tutors and mentors,
- If possible, hire a TA to respond to students,
- Try to immediately acknowledge the receipt of a student's question, and set a period of time in which feedback will be returned.

ONLINE TEACHING IN COMPUTER WORLD

Welcome to the first of at least two reports related to instruction on the Internet. The aim of this particular report, "Online Teaching in an Online World," is to understand the online learning experiences, obstacles, supports, and preferences of college instructors across a variety of institutional settings and disciplines.

Whereas this initial report focuses on the online learning needs and supports of higher education faculty, the second study, "Online

Training in an Online World," addresses similar issues in the corporate training world. After detailing the survey results and conclusions, a set of recommendations are proposed related to online learning in higher education settings.

Perhaps no technology has so swiftly assumed prominence in both educational and commercial settings as the Web. In educational arenas, those who previously found higher education too expensive or physically inaccessible can now access a myriad of online information resources and materials. Ideas and feedback from online expert guests, mentors, and peers are now available in college classes. Finnish instructors and students can collaborate with those in the United States and Korea. Online student mentoring can come from practitioners in the field, experts at the North Pole, or graduate students and colleagues down the hall. Collaborative teaming in online college settings knows no bounds, and, not surprisingly, higher education administrators have taken notice. As a result, new instructional expectations for college faculty are emerging. This survey targeted instructors who were likely to have greater experience with these new teaching methods and tools than others. This final report is intended to provide insights into the future directions of online teaching as well as to identify the gaps in tool and courseware development efforts.

Previous Reports

A report from the Web-based Education Commission indicates that Web technologies are increasingly used in both online and traditional classroom-based courses. This report also notes that distance learning course offerings are expected to increase from 62 per cent of four-year colleges offering some courses online in 1998 to 84 per cent of such colleges offering such online course experiences in 2002. As a result, the Commission notes that many higher education institutions are forming consortia and collaborative groups to share course materials and resources in an effort to enhance college teaching and learning.

In terms of specific Web tools, the commission reports a dramatic increase in college faculty utilizing e-mail, Web resources, course homepages, and online discussions within their courses. In fact, they report a 25 per cent increase from 1996 to 1999 in college faculty utilizing Web resources in their class syllabi.

This report also acknowledges the additional time and risk on the part of faculty who attempt to take advantage of online learning tools and activities in their courses. But why is there a risk? Higher education institutions simply do not yet have the teaching rewards, expectations, or support structures in place for promoting faculty teaching in an online world. As e-learning environments take centre stage in college programmes around the world, it is vital to determine the tools and tasks that facilitate student learning in this new context as well as to establish quality standards for such courses. A recent report from the Institute for Higher Education Policy that was commissioned by the National Education Association and Blackboard, Inc. identified 24 key benchmarks for online learning quality.

These benchmarks addressed course development guidelines, instructional material reviews, student feedback and interaction, access to library resources, technical support, student advising procedures, and the evaluation of intended learning outcomes. There are a number of other summary reports attempting to describe and evaluate the use of distance education technology in education.

Some reports speak to the challenges of teaching in an online world, including issues of compensation, time, ownership, profitability, training, technology infrastructure, and university policies. Jaffee for instance, discusses the costs of online instruction as well as the forms of resistance to such courses and programmes at both the institutional and individual level. Others point to new economic markets and opportunities. Such reports document key trends, social demographics, stakeholders, policy makers, major players, and workplace needs. Still other reports detail newly formed and tenuous partnerships and consortia. What about the instructional, psychological, and social aspects of online learning? At least one report has been commissioned to develop guidelines or benchmarks – including many instructional design guidelines – to ensure quality distance education practices.

On the social and psychological side of online learning, Joseph Walther and his colleagues point to the social issues embedded in online environments such as student social isolation and shared knowledge.

In a more recent report, Bonk and Wisher summarize the research related to online collaborative tools, e-learning, the role of the instructor, and the increasing importance of learner-centred approaches to instruction.

They also suggest more than two dozen psychologically-based research opportunities in online collaboration related to principles of cognition, motivation, social interaction, and individual differences. Within the plethora of distance education reports and prophecies, the TeleLearning Network Centres of Excellence of Canada have assumed a leadership role related to online learning research. One of their key reports compares eight key post-secondary institutions offering e-learning. In this report, Massey and Curry provide a preliminary analysis of universities emerging in this field such as Stanford University, Nova Southeastern, Western Governors University, Indiana University, the University of Illinois, Open University UK, University of Phoenix Online, and California Virtual University.

They offer a competitive analysis of the courses/programmes, pedagogy, and learner support structures in place at each of these institutions. In addition, they address expansion plans, marketing, faculty, learners/clients, and course production and delivery mechanisms at each institution. As such, this particular report offers useful insights into the direction of online technologies and course delivery.

While the TeleLearning NCE is a source for online learning reports from Canada, UCLA has recently published an inaugural report on the impact of the Internet on social, political, cultural, and economic behaviour and ideas across the United States. While that research investigates Internet usage across the general population of the United States, the data in the present study focus on evaluations of Internet usage in college courses among college instructors likely to use it.

Current Tension

There is no doubt that the Internet has brought about a new forum for learning and instruction. Higher education faculty and administrators must not only understand the new technologies that present themselves, but they also must grapple with how best to utilize them for student learning. Or as Steven Gilbert recently noted, "Acquiring the knowledge and skill necessary to improve teaching and learning with technology requires faculty, support professionals, and administrators to think and behave in new ways—deep learning." The challenge, he argues, is for early adopters of technology to push at the educational frontiers in ways that help transform themselves as well as their colleagues with new insights and lifelong learning, while staying within the educational missions and resources of their respective institutions.

But on college campuses there is tension and uncertainty surrounding the use of the Internet in teaching and learning. There is also a lot of hype. Free classes mentioned one day are delayed by downturns in the economy the next. Standards and guidelines are encouraged, but too often not established. Distance learning policies created one year are revamped in the years that follow. Moreover, too many reports speak from an administrator, politician, or corporate executive viewpoint. What is often lacking is a sense of what the faculty member or instructor thinks about the online experience. As a result, few reports reflect on the pedagogical practices that lead to online learning success.

It is as if the technology alone is sufficient to build an effective environment for learning. And this, we know, is not the case. Few can doubt that Web-based teaching and learning is a growing field with rapid changes. In part, it has emerged to fill the void in training as technical skills quickly fall into obsolescence. Reskilling simply is a fact of life. Online reskilling may be a necessity as the age of learners increases and the time available for one's studies is curtailed by job and family responsibilities. Web-based courses may simply be the only viable option for many learners.

The present study attempts to determine the supports and resources that college faculty have available to meet those needs.

Whereas other surveys of online learning in higher education have explored areas such as technological resource availability, instructor skills and attitudes, or institutional policies, this particular study is more comprehensive by attempting to understand instructor attitudes, experiences, preferences, and online support structures, as well as prevalent pedagogical tools and practices. Given this focus, the results of this survey can perhaps help educators design more powerful e-learning environments as well as methods to teach within them. Hopefully, it will serve as a barometer for higher education institutions considering online courses and programmes as well as a guidepost for instructors first encountering online teaching in this online world.

Focus on Pedagogical Practices

There is no doubt that Web-based instruction offers new ways for students to collaborate and for instructors to share pedagogical ideas and practices. It is also a way to expand the resources available to students and build permanent course archives. With the emergence of the Web, it is now possible to involve practitioners, experts, and peers as online learning guides or mentors. Case-based learning can take on a new sense of authenticity as business students chat with company executives, counseling students reflect online about crisis situations faced during internships, preservice teachers peek in on the classroom management strategies of expert teachers, and medical students virtually view sophisticated operations in action.

There seem to be limitless opportunities to exploit the Web in college teaching and learning. As online learning resources accumulate and become archived, there is even a new sense of course history and legacy. Events that were delivered or that unfolded a decade or more ago can be replayed, modified, salvaged, contemplated, and debated at any time. As a result of all these new instructional opportunities, the decisions confronting the online college instructors are multiplied. Part of this is due to the complexity of these environments that often beg for quick managerial decision making one minute, technological expertise the next, and social or pedagogical intervention just a few moments later.

This survey will help document some of the early pedagogical practices of those deciding to teach online, or, at least, those beginning to utilize online resources somewhere in their teaching practices.

Purpose of the Study

This report is based on a survey of 222 college faculty members, most of whom have been early adopters of Webbased technology in their instruction. Unlike some of the previous studies, online course quality is just one aspect of this particular report. In addition, this survey report is intended to inform administrators and courseware designers of the benefits and challenges of using Web-based learning tools in higher education settings.

It also provides suggestions about the types of tools, activities, resources, and support structures that might enhance online learning in college settings. This survey report provides descriptive information about the types of college instructors and institutions involved in typical online environments.

It has five primary goals:

- To identify the resources, tools, and activities that college instructors desire in their Web-based teaching efforts;
- To document the gaps between online teaching practices and preferences;
- To understand some of the key obstacles as well as support structures for Web-based teaching in college settings;
- To point to online learning tools and communities that might be developed to enhance teaching and learning in higher education settings; and,
- To determine who is responsible for making online learning decisions in higher education.

In effect, this study intends to document how faculty educators are being trained, supported, and rewarded for online instruction. It also seeks to determine the types of online tools and activities that faculty prefer. Additionally, this survey explores college instructor attitudes related to online learning obstacles and support. It addresses their perceptions of controversial online learning issues such as course ownership and quality, online programme accreditation, online teaching and learning opportunities, and the general utility of the Web as a teaching and learning resource.

The conclusions are intended to help those teaching in online environments as well as those developing policies and funding new online initiatives. The findings may also be useful to companies developing and evaluating online tools for distance teaching and learning.

Methodological Overview

As distance learning tensions rise in response to concerns about online pedagogy and policy, we need to understand more from faculty who have crossed some of the first hurdles.

Where can one go to look for the early adopters or at least those who are less resistant to incorporating the Web in their teaching? Who are the ones to ask about online teaching practices? While previous research indicates that college instructors too often are not utilizing the most sophisticated technologies and interaction opportunities, nevertheless, faculty members were considered ideal sources for providing information on Web-based teaching policies, experiences, training, and incentives in higher education. In this report, we sampled college instructors who had a history of sharing resources on the Web.

Sampling Procedures

Our sampling of instructors employing the Web for teaching and learning purposes comes from two separate sources. First, we selected a random sample of names from The World Lecture Hall. The WLH is an international site first created in 1994 at the University of Texas at Austin to post college syllabi for courses within a variety of academic disciplines. The developers have received national praise and recognition for offering this service.

When beginning to select that sample, however, we noticed the emergence of another resource for faculty and students in higher education. MERLOT was created in 1997 by the California State University Centre for Distributed Learning. It has since expanded to consortia of other institutions and state systems. MERLOT is now a fast growing and free resource intended as an online community of shared knowledge and ideas. In contrast to the WLH, the MERLOT site was originally designed for sharing a wide variety of online learning materials, including assignments, reviews, and member profiles across many academic disciplines within higher education. The capability for peer instructors to review online learning materials was the key feature that distinguished MERLOT from other online resource sharing sites at the time of this study. Even though the WLH and MERLOT members are not representative of all college faculty members, they provide richer online learning backgrounds and experiences than most other available populations. Over 2000 syllabi reflecting more than 80 disciplines and subdisciplines have been posted to the WLH.

Those posting syllabi to the WLH include faculty from religious studies, sociology, theater and dance, accounting, philosophy, marketing, zoology, history, neuroscience, astronomy, nutrition, anthropology, rhetoric, law, and electrical engineering.

At the time of this study, MERLOT contained over 2000 members representing more than 120 different disciplines. Members of MERLOT include faculty from such disciplines as nursing, teacher education, business information systems, geology, arts, computer science, political science, evolution, and theoretical mathematics. The combined sample population, therefore, included a variety of disciplines, degree programmes, and types and sizes of institutions. It also included a wide range of Web expertise.

All these people, however, either had experience posting syllabi online or posting online profiles, critiques, or learning materials. For some in the sample, however, this may have been just a one-time post or brief comment.

While the WLH and MERLOT were perhaps the most well known Web sites for resource sharing within higher education at the time of this study, we were not aware of surveys of college faculty representing either or both of these sites. Our random sample during November and early December 2000 included 415 instructors from MERLOT and 286 from the WLH, or a total of 701 instructors from a wide spectrum of disciplines at both sites.1 From e-mail solicitations to this sample, we collected 222 completed surveys; the vast majority were faculty or administrators with additional college teaching responsibilities.

While our 32 per cent response rate was generally lower than direct mail or phone surveys, online survey research suggests that this rate is quite good.

However, at this time, no expected response rate for online surveys has been firmly established. Nearly fifty different disciplines and subdisciplines were represented in our final sample. Most responses were received from instructors from across the United States, though around 5 per cent of the respondents came from other countries including Hong Kong, Australia, Canada, and the United Kingdom.

Limitations of the Study

As with most online surveys, the present project had several limitations that may have constrained the results and generalizability of the study:

- There are few available resources for faculty online course-sharing, thereby limiting the selection to two of the more popular sites, the WLH and MERLOT. These two Web sites were possibly not representative of all college faculty members who use the Web in their teaching.
- Since users created these sites over long periods of time, many of the collected online faculty member names and e-mail addresses were outdated, incorrect, or changed, especially those in the World Lecture Hall.
- Many of the faculty respondents here were Web savvy and could be described as early adopters of Web technology, thereby inflating any optimistic results regarding online learning experiences and felt need for additional online collaborative tools compared to college faculty in general.
- Tools for teaching and learning on the Web are constantly changing. As a result, it is difficult to generalize many of the findings of this survey related to the utility of particular Web-based instructional tools.
- The online survey instrument was relatively lengthy,

effectively lowering the response rate and perhaps causing some inaccurate or skipped responses.

- This survey report labels respondents as college or post-secondary instructors, even though a few of the respondents were in administrative positions with only part-time faculty or teaching responsibilities.
- In an effort to keep the survey at a manageable length, the online survey failed to address key issues such as how courseware tools are funded, the per cent of respondents with tenure, the perceived quality of online certificates or institutes, the forms of online training for instructors, the types of technical support provided for students and faculty working online, how costs are determined for online courses, and perceived learning and motivational factors in online learning. It is hoped that future studies will address such issues.

Despite these limitations, the response rate for this online survey was higher than expected for an e-mail solicited Web survey. In fact, only 7 per cent of those solicited in this particular survey explicitly refused to participate.

Respondent Background

Description of Survey Respondents

Nearly 64 per cent of our sample came from MERLOT, while 36 per cent were from the WLH. In addition, the response rate was slightly higher for MERLOT participants as compared to WLH participants. These differences in response rate are due, in part, to MERLOT being a recent phenomenon with a more current faculty listing.

Type and Size of Respondent Institution

National studies indicate that distance education is more prevalent in public than private institutions and in 4-year rather than 2- year institutions. Not surprisingly, then, it appears that college instructors who are active in posting resources to the Web are from those types of institutions. In this particular study, over two-thirds of our respondents were from public institutions. Only 1 per cent came from 2-year private institutions and 20 per cent from 4-year private institutions.

Nine per cent of the respondents were employed in other types of instructional situations or indicated that they were in a public or private college setting but without noting whether it was a 2-year or 4-year institution. Respondents were three times more likely to be from 4-year than 2-year institutions. The type and size of institutions ranged from large Research I institutions such as the University of Texas at Austin, Arizona State University, the University of Illinois, and the University of Maryland College Park to more modestly-sized state colleges such as Indiana State University, Northern Michigan University, the University of Wisconsin Whitewater, and the University of Akron, to small private institutions such as St. Norbert College, Oberlin College, Nazareth College, and Belmont Abbey College.

As indicated by reports from the National Centre for Education Statistics and the National Educational Association, distance education is often linked to institutional size. In those previous studies, distance learning faculty members were more likely to work at larger institutions. Additionally, distance education courses were more likely to be taught at the larger institutions. In this study, more than 50 per cent of the survey participants were from large institutions. In contrast, approximately 20 per cent were from small institutions that had enrollments of less than 3,000. Slightly more than onefourth of the respondents were from medium-sized institutions.

Years of College Teaching Experience

In addition to the institution the participants represented, we also were interested in their teaching experiences. Unlike the NEA study which found that distance learning faculty members tended to be younger and have fewer years of teaching experience, the present study found that college instructors who are willing to share resources online tended to be older and more established. While 30 per cent had 10 or fewer years of experience teaching college, 34 per cent had 11 to 20 years of experience, and around

36 per cent had more than 20 years of experience.

This is an important finding since it reveals that Web-based instructional role models can be found across generations of faculty. It also indicates that there are many established college instructors who can mentor incoming faculty in Web-based practices and experiences. As will be pointed out later in this report, established faculty may have more time available to explore online teaching methods and do so at significantly lower risk.

Age of Respondents

Based on the research mentioned previously from the NEA, it was expected that younger faculty members would be sharing resources online more often than older instructors. Surprisingly, nearly half of our respondents were over age 51. Fewer than 7 per cent were under age 36. These data are somewhat surprising given the conventional wisdom that the Internet is dominated by younger age groups and that older faculty members tend to be more reluctant to use technologies in their instruction. This finding is in contrast to a UCLA report that computer use is nearly double a source of stress for faculty over the age of 45 than for those younger than 35. Nevertheless, the more recent survey on Internet usage from UCLA also indicated all age groups now utilize the Internet. Even the 2 per cent of Web users over age 65 in the present study is quite heartening.

Gender of Respondents

Nearly 60 per cent of the WLH or MERLOT respondents were male. Given the gender-related trends of the past few decades related to both computer experience and use favouring boys and higher education employment figures favouring males, this is not too surprising. The gender representation in this sample is reflective of commonly cited gender patterns of higher education faculty.

Faculty Rank

The recent NEA study revealed that distance education and traditional faculty have similar educational backgrounds, professorial ranks or positions and tenure status. In the NEA study, 36 per cent of those teaching distance education courses were lecturers and another 7 per cent were unranked, or about 43 per cent of the total.

In contrast, in the present study, lecturers represented fewer than 5 per cent of those posting to the WLH or MERLOT and adjunct professors accounted for another 8 per cent. In effect, the WLH and MERLOT seem to attract very few lecturers and adjunct instructors.

Ten per cent of the respondents in this study were classified as "other". So while the NEA data clearly indicated that lecturers and unranked faculty members are involved in Web-based instruction, they are not typically sharing their work electronically with other college faculty in two of the most prominent course-sharing sites—the WLH and MERLOT. And, in contrast to the large unranked or lecturer population in the NEA study, most respondents here were in professorial ranks.

Educational Background

Our sample also differed from the NEA study in terms of educational backgrounds of the participants. In the NEA study, about half of the respondents had master's degrees but only 30 per cent had a Ph.D. or Ed.D. In our study, in contrast, 70 per cent of the sample had a Ph.D. or Ed.D. and another 6 per cent were ABD, while just 22 per cent had a master's as their highest degree held. Thus, college faculty members involved in sharing course resources online appear to have more extensive educational backgrounds than other distance education faculty. The determinants of these differences are unknown.

Level of Courses Taught

It was also deemed useful to find out what type of courses these instructors taught. Given the amount of negative press about the lack of undergraduate level involvement of college faculty from Research I institutions, it was encouraging that almost all respondents had undergraduate teaching experience. Still, more than 60 per cent had taught at the graduate level. Perhaps most interestingly, over forty per cent had taught non-credit or other types of courses such as workshops, enrichment programmes, or training courses.

Participation in Online Course Sharing

When Do They Share

The emergence of online course sharing is a relatively new phenomenon. In fact, 54 per cent of respondents first posted to one these two Web sites— the WLH and MERLOT—within the past year, and an additional 17 per cent within the past two years. The remaining 29 per cent indicated that they posted more than two years ago. While these numbers are reflective of how long these sites have been available, a culture of sharing online resources seems to be emerging.

It might be the case that sites such as the WLH and MERLOT have simply become more popular among faculty during the year leading up to this study. Or, perhaps, sufficient Internet access and speed finally exists for college faculty to share resources online.

How Did They Discover Sharing Resources

We were interested in finding out how the college faculty members discovered sites for sharing resources online. Thus, we inquired as to how they heard about the WLH or MERLOT resources. Fewer than 5 per cent had heard about them through advertisements, and, surprisingly, none listed a friend as an important source. More typically, they had learned about these resources through their institution, a colleague, an Internet link, or through other means such as mailing lists, journal objects, special interest groups, or conferences. Thus, the most effective communication channels were professional contracts or electronic communications.

Why Share

In addition to asking how the faculty respondents in our study were informed of these resources for online course sharing, we asked why they posted to these sites. Around 8 per cent responded that their institution or department required them to do so. Approximately twice as many respondents claimed to have posted to these sites as a means of marketing themselves to other colleagues.

About the same number indicated that they posted to one of these sites as a pedagogical experiment, while another 16 per cent became active in the site for fun.

Thirty-eight per cent of those posting simply wanted to share pedagogical theories or strategies with their colleagues. Slightly more were active in one or more of these sites in order to grow as professionals.

The most frequently selected response was that they simply believed in the importance of course sharing. Around 18 per cent gave other reasons for their affiliations to the WLH or MERLOT. For instance, several respondents noted that they were asked by Merlot officials to join, while a few others indicated that someone else posted their name or information.

Type and Number of Resulting Contacts

We also inquired about the type and number of contacts that these faculty respondents received as a result of posting resources or information to one of these two Web sites. Of the faculty completing this item, sixty-one per cent were contacted by others after sharing their syllabus or profile on the Web. The data here are varied and interesting.

Twelve per cent of the respondents had been contacted by researchers, while nearly three times as many were contacted by other instructors. In addition, more then 30 per cent had been contacted by students not in their courses.

Interestingly, 14 per cent had been contacted by publishers and 12 per cent by other companies and institutions. Such findings reveal the marketing and networking potential of online resource sharing. Not only are students attracted to one's class after reading an online syllabus, but textbook publishers, researchers, and other institutions are also knocking on one's door. We were interested in determining the average number of contacts for each group described previously. Whereas contacts by publishers, institutions, and other companies were relatively infrequent, a number of people indicated that they had been contacted by students or instructors more than ten times as a result of their online resource contribution or membership.

Perhaps it is the course marketing and enhanced collegiality that instructors find most appealing about these course-sharing resources. In fact, more than ninety per cent indicated that comments from colleagues on their syllabus or other posted course resources would be helpful.

6

Function of E-learning Development

A wide variety of models of e learning have been proposed, which concentrate on different aspects of the development life cycle, and there is a substantial literature on the subject. However the vast majority of this work starts from the point at which the course has already been decided and concentrates on the development and delivery of the course. By contrast there is very little about determining what courses should be selected in relation to institutional strategic plans, and there is little to help course developers determine which parts of the course are best supported by e learning and which by other forms of learning.

It is worth looking at some of the guidelines and benchmarks that have been devised for the development of e learning courses and consider these in relation to our model. Here we find that there are few examples of models which do take into account the institutional context. For instance The Institute for Higher Education Policy lists five benchmarks for institutional support (IHEP 2000):

1. Faculty are provided professional incentives for innovative practices to encourage development of distance learning courses.
2. There are institutional rewards for the effective teaching of distance learning courses.
3. A documented technology plan is in place to ensure quality standards.

4. Electronic security measures are in place to ensure the integrity and validity of information.
5. Support for building and maintaining the distance education infrastructure is addressed by a centralized system.

These refer to institutional support for developing and maintaining the course but do not consider how the course relates to institutional strategy. In broad terms the IHEP finds focus particularly on some (institutional) aspects of development and teaching. They include also aspects of planning and, by extension, the guides on teaching relate also to learning.

The American Council for Education gives 5 guiding principles which they say are not a "how-to", but "a statement designed to address the qualities that should characterize the learning society in the years ahead" (ACE 1997).

- **Learning Design**: Distance learning activities are designed to fit the specific context for learning.
- **Learner Support**: Distance learning opportunities are effectively supported for learners through fully accessible modes of delivery and resources.
- **Organisational Commitment**: Distance learning initiatives must be backed by an organizational commitment to quality and effectiveness in all aspects of the learning environment.
- **Learning Outcomes**: Distance learning programs organize learning around demonstrable learning outcomes, assist the learner to achieve these outcomes, and assess learner progress by reference to these outcomes.
- **Technology**: The provider has a plan and infrastructure for using technology that supports its learning goals and activities.

The ACE model deals with a restricted part of the full development life cycle model. It covers aspects of design and learning and some aspects of planning in relation to design but does not deal with development, teaching and critically does not deal with review. Turning to the UK there are several bodies working in the same area, and it is worth looking at two of them;

the Open and Distance Learning Quality Council (ODLQC) and the Quality Assurance Agency (QAA). The ODLQC defines ten areas for its standards:

1. Course Outcomes
2. Course Contents
3. Publicity & Recruitment
4. Admission Procedures
5. Learning Support
6. Open Learning Centres
7. Learner Welfare
8. The Provider
9. Joint Provision
10. Accreditation.

The ODLQC focuses on planning teaching and learning aspects including aspects of review. It does not deal with design or development. The QAA has, at the time of writing, published two documents of relevance here: its distance learning guidelines which are divided into six guidelines and 23 precepts and its (draft) Code of practice for the assurance of academic quality and standards in higher education. The areas covered in the distance learning guidelines are:

- System design - the development of an integrated approach
- The establishment of academic standards and quality in programme design, approval and review procedures
- The assurance of quality and standards in the management of programme delivery
- Student development and support
- Student communication and representation
- Student assessment

As can be seen these are primarily concerned with the development and delivery of the course from the point at which it has been decided to develop it. The QAA does however look at some of the institutional aspects of this, with three of its first four precepts (2, 3 and 4) having an institutional rather than course focus (QAA n.d.):

- The provision of programmes of study by distance learning should form part of an explicit strategy for achieving an institution's stated aims, and the distance learning system or systems should be designed and developed in ways that will give effect to the strategy.
- Prior to offering programmes of study by distance learning, an institution should explicitly design and test its system for administering and teaching students at a distance and plan for contingencies in order to meet its stated aims in terms of academic quality and standards.
- An institution should safeguard its position in respect of the law in any country in which it is proposed that programmes of study should be made available by distance learning.

Of particular interest is the first precept quoted above which points out that distance learning needs to be related to the institution's aims. This precept however is about whether distance learning is compatible with the institution's aims, and does not consider whether the course itself is compatible with the stated aims of the institution; again this is assumed to be so.

The areas covered in the Code of practice for the assurance of academic quality and standards in higher education which covered collaborative and flexible distance learning include issues associated with governance such as

- Responsibility for, and equivalence of, academic standards.
- Policies, procedures and information.
- Selecting a partner organisation or agent.
- Written agreements with a partner organisation or agent.
- Assuring academic standards and the quality of programmes and awards.
- Assessment requirements. etc.

There is an implicit model within this, but it is primarily concerned with quality assurance and the nature of the partnerships between institutions in the case of collaborative learning, and has nothing to say about how courses are created and developed beyond. One model that deals with the full cycle is that of the

Western Cooperative for Educational Telecommunications (WCET) (WCET 2000) which raises as the first issue in its guidelines and protocols how the course aligns with the institution's mission: In its content, purposes, organization, and enrolment history if applicable, the program is consistent with the institution's role and mission.

It goes on to expand upon this by asking:

- "What is the evidence that the program is consistent with the role and mission of the institution including its goals with regard to student access?
- Is the institution fulfilling its stated role as it offers the program to students at a distance, or is the role being changed? "

As such this offers a good point to start for defining an e learning life-cycle model for the development of e learning. The areas defined in the Commissioners guidelines are:

- Institutional context and commitment
- Curriculum and instruction
- Faculty support
- Student support
- Evaluation and assessment

These areas can be seen to focus on the learning, review and planning aspects but in details link also the design, development and the teaching processes.

Institutional Models of Learning Processes

There is a need to consider the models of learning which are embodied in institutional processes (implicit and explicit). Like the models these may concentrate only on particular parts of the process, though they embody a different set of processes since they are typically focused on the quality assurance requirements that institutions need to demonstrate the validity of the course. There is some variation in the models used, in part related to the scale of activities with concomitant difference in procedures and in part due to the interpretation of guidelines by different institutional administrations. However the principles remain fairly constant, so it is worth looking at what they typically cover, and equally what they do not cover.

Any proposed model for the development of e learning has to be capable of incorporating the current practice that is mandatory at universities for the development, approval, delivery and review of courses. However, as this chapter demonstrates there are considerable gaps in existing formal processes which in part reflect historical practices.

Most of the existing models were developed for traditional teaching techniques and have been refined over many years to meet particular accreditation needs, for which they have been seen deemed sufficient. However, in many cases these formal processes are augmented by informal processes that reflect other needs within the institution. These formal and informal processes may not be enough for the development of e learning, as e learning makes many issues transparent which before had been opaque or hidden.

Proposed Model

There is a need for a model that encompasses all stages in e learning from determining which courses to develop through their development, delivery and review to their ultimate decommissioning. Such a model is necessary if an effective evaluation system is to be designed and run. Since evaluation needs to look at the dependencies between aspects of the life cycle, such as design, delivery and student performance, in order that observation at one stage can trigger action at another, then a full life cycle model is *sine qua non*. An incomplete model can be argued on first principles to exclude any such evaluation set up. Currently there are no suitable models, which means that we have had to develop a new one. The focus of this model is to support evaluation to ensure that the courses developed meet the various stakeholder needs. It is expected that over time each part of the model will be further elaborated, often using existing models to provide the necessary detail. It should be remembered that what follows is a model of the life cycle and not a set of step by step instructions.

The model has six phases, though these overlap and in real development processes there will be feedback and complex dependencies as described later. The six phases are divided into three groups:

- Review and Planning
- Review
- Planning
- Curriculum development
- Course design
- Course development
- Delivery
- Teaching
- Student learning.

For each of these phases the most important external drivers and controls and the critical processes are shown. The drivers and controls are those forces which place parameters and restrictions on what can be done. They should not be considered immovable, however they are unlikely to be significantly changeable in the short term. Clearly, feedback from all stages of the planning, development, delivery and review should be one of the influences on both the internal and external drivers, but the life-cycle for these is generally much longer than for the development of courses.

It is necessary to look at each of these phases before considering how and where to evaluate them and how these evaluations feed back in to other aspects of the life cycle where action can be taken.

Expanding the model

There has been space only to discuss the model very briefly at the top level, and not to look inside each of the areas in any detail. Clearly expansion is necessary; especially for the areas that are to be studied in detail. There is not sufficient space here to give a full exposition of the table, and we will therefore look at a single column in detail. Also, it is important to recognise that the ideas set out here are in a process of development and it would be wrong to give the impression that they are worked out in detail or that there is a single way of looking at these issues. Since we believe, that planning is the critical stage to focus research on at the moment we have chosen to expand our initial ideas this one stage further purely to demonstrate the need for this.

Planning

This will always be the first concrete phase of any new course, but will typically build on the reviews of previous courses as well. One thing that this model does not attempt to address is where ideas for new or updated courses come from.

The starting point could be from individual lecturers who wish to develop a course related to their interests, from a department reviewing its portfolio of courses and identifying areas which it wants to strengthen, from pressure from students, from regulatory bodies (an example here would be the way in which the General Medical Council (GMC) revised the medical curriculum forcing institutions to re-develop many of their medical courses) or from some planning function. Traditionally a supply driven model has predominated in the UK sector, but this has already led to course failures across the e learning world, and a demand driven model is now seen as necessary. Failure to adequately understand demand will likely lead to failure in course provision.

Controls and Drivers

Until relatively recently it has been rare in higher education for courses to be mapped against the institution's mission and strategic plan. In many cases courses are developed either because of external drivers (such as the GMC) or because of the interests of particular members of staff. However, given the greater constraints on funding and increasing need for institutions to concentrate on their strengths there is a need to move towards planning the entire portfolio of courses against institutional strategy. This becomes much more obvious with the growth of e learning since e-learning tends to make many issues more transparent. In particular e-learning developments show the need both to separate out aspects of the life cycle and to connect parts of the life cycle together. Such transparency in the life cycle and its processes will help, for instance, to determine which areas are critical for the development of e learning courses, or the migration of existing courses into an e learning framework.

Institutional Capacity

Institutional capacity has many dimensions including:

- Staff availability and capacity; their skill level in the subject matter, pedagogy and e learning
- Learning resources; electronic and library resources and laboratory or other equipment as necessary. This, of course, raises particular issues where learning is distributed. The Open University has a long tradition of "kitchen table science" by developing experiments which can be done at home.
- Learning support; Each additional course taken on adds to the load on learning support; and the form that this takes varies between courses, but is generally different for e learning courses with, for instance, a greater need for technical support.
- Administrative capacity to support marketing, enrolment etc.
- Technology infrastructure; e learning has specific requirements.

Learner Outcomes and Goals

From a data definition perspective, learner goals and learner outcomes differ primarily in that goals are specified prior to the learning experience, while outcomes are generally determined after the learning experience. Higher education has long struggled with the definitional, analytical, and measurement issues related to student outcomes. E-learning will heighten the importance of addressing these issues in two significant ways.

First, e-learning provides students a greater opportunity to pursue a wider variety of student-defined goals. Students will not be constrained to develop levels of skills and knowledge that are institutionally defined and packaged in prescribed programs. This means that student outcomes will need to be defined in ways that are consistent with student goals, and, perhaps more important, information about student goals and outcomes will need to be obtained directly from students. This does not imply, however, that outcomes defined from an institutional perspective will become less important; it simply adds another dimension to data systems.

Second, it may be possible to overcome some of the problems of measuring participation and learner-provider interaction by turning to measuring learner outcomes. Participation measures are currently used as proxies for outcomes in many policy development and decision-making contexts. In the long run, it may be easier, and even necessary, to look beyond time-on-task metrics to measuring outcomes and competencies, particularly in the case of asynchronous delivery modes.

Many efforts have been made to define the outcomes of higher education, often from different perspectives or to support different policy purposes. A good point of departure for data system development related to goals and outcomes is a taxonomy that Patrick Terenzini developed, drawing on historical work.

E-LEARNING (THEORY) AND PRINCIPLES

E-learning theory describes the cognitive science principles of effective multimedia e-learning. Cognitive research and theory suggest that selection of appropriate concurrent multimedia modalities may enhance learning, as may application of several other principles.

Richard E. Mayer's "modality principle" states that if materials contain both verbal and graphical information, the verbal information should be given in auditory format only, and not as written text as well.

Theoretically, the modality principle is based on a model of working memory by Alan Baddeley and Graham Hitch who proposed that working memory has two largely independent sub-components that tend to work in parallel - one visual and one verbal/acoustic. This gave rise to dual-coding theory, first proposed by Allan Paivio and later applied to multimedia by Richard Mayer. According to Mayer, separate channels of working memory process auditory and visual information. Consequently, a learner can use more cognitive processing capacities to study materials that combine auditory verbal information with visual graphical information than to process materials that combine printed (visual) text with visual graphical information. In other words, the multi modal materials reduce the cognitive load imposed on working memory.

In a series of studies Mayer and his colleagues tested Paivio's dual-coding theory, with multimedia. They repeatedly found that students learning given multimedia with animation and narration consistently did better on transfer questions than those who learn from animation and text-based materials. That is, they were significantly better when it came to applying what they had learned after receiving multimedia rather than mono-media (visual only) instruction. These results were then later confirmed by other groups of researchers.

The initial studies of multimedia learning were limited to logical scientific processes that centered on cause-and-effect systems like automobile braking systems, how a bicycle pump works, or cloud formation. However, subsequent investigations found that the modality effect extended to other areas of learning.

Split attention effect Mayer found that "Students learn better from animation and narration than from animation, narration, and on-screen text."

Thus, it is better to eliminate redundant material. Learners do not learn as well when they both hear and see the same verbal message during a presentation. This is a special case of the split attention effect of Sweller and Chandler.

Learning is enhanced when related components such as words and pictures are presented in "spatial contiguity", referring to the components being physically close to each other on the page or screen, rather than being separated. Similarly, "temporal contiguity" refers to simultaneous presentation of corresponding words and pictures, rather than successive delivery. Learning is more effective when extraneous material is excluded rather than included, which Meyer termed, "coherence". The effects of improved design have more benefit for low-knowledge than high knowledge learners, and for high-spatial than for low-spatial learners.

Such principles may not apply outside of laboratory conditions. For example, Muller found that adding approximately 50% additional extraneous but interesting material did not result in any significant difference in learner performance. There is on-going debate concerning the mechanisms underlying these beneficial principles, and on what boundary conditions may apply.

Learning Theories

Good pedagogical practice has a theory of learning at its core. However, no single best-practice e-learning standard has emerged, and may be unlikely given the range of learning and teaching styles, the potential ways technology can be implemented and the ways in which educational technology itself is changing. Various pedagogical approaches or learning theories may be considered in designing and interacting with e-learning programs.

Social-constructivist - this pedagogy is particularly well afforded by the use of discussion forums, blogs, wiki and on-line collaborative activities. It is a collaborative approach that opens educational content creation to a wider group including the students themselves. The One Laptop Per Child Foundation attempted to use a constructivist approach in its project.

Laurillard's Conversational Model is also particularly relevant to eLearning, and Gilly Salmon's Five-Stage Model is a pedagogical approach to the use of discussion boards.

Cognitive perspective focuses on the cognitive processes involved in learning as well as how the brain works.

Emotional perspective focuses on the emotional aspects of learning, like motivation, engagement, fun, etc.

Behavioural perspective focuses on the skills and behavioural outcomes of the learning process. Role-playing and application to on-the-job settings.

Contextual perspective focuses on the environmental and social aspects which can stimulate learning. Interaction with other people, collaborative discovery and the importance of peer support as well as pressure.

Mode Neutral Convergence or promotion of 'transmodal' learning where online and classroom learners can coexist within one learning environment thus encouraging interconnectivity and the harnessing of collective intelligence. For many theorists it's the interaction between student and teacher and student and student in the online environment that enhances learning (Mayes and de Freitas 2004). Pask's theory that learning occurs through conversations about a subject which in turn helps to make knowledge explicit has an obvious application to learning within aVLE.

Salmon developed a five stage model of e-learning and e-moderating that for some time has had a major influence where online courses and online discussion forums have been used. In her five stage model individual access and the ability of students to use the technology are the first step to involvement and achievement. The second step involves students creating an identity online and finding others with whom to interact; online socialisation is a critical element of the e-learning process in this model. In step 3 students are giving and sharing information relevant to the course to each other. Collaborative interaction amongst students is central to step 4. The fifth step in Salmon's model involves students looking for benefits from the system and using resources from outside of it to deepen their learning. Throughout all of this the tutor/teacher/lecturer fulfills the role of moderator or e-moderator, acting as a facilitator of student learning.

Some criticism is now beginning to emerge. Her model does not easily transfer to other contexts (she developed it with experience from an Open University distance learning course). It ignores the variety of learning approaches that are possible within computer mediated communication (CMC) and the range of learning theories that are available (Moule 2007).

Self-regulation

Self-regulated learning refers to several concepts that play major roles in learning, and which have significant relevance in e-learning. Zimmerman (1998) emphasizes that for students to develop self-regulation, learning courses should offer opportunities for them to practice these strategies and skills by themselves. Also self-regulation relates to social sources such as parents and teachers as well. Moreover, Steinberg (1996) found out that high-achieving students usually have high-expectation parents who monitor their children closely.

With the academic environment, self-regulated learner usually set their academic goals and monitor and react themselves in process in order to achieve their goals. Schunk argues, "students must regulate not only their actions but also their underlying achievement-related cognitions, beliefs, intentions and affects". Moreover, academic self-regulation helps students develop their confidence to perform well on learning courses.

THE FUNCTION OF THE E-LEARNING MODEL

Many models of e learning have been proposed for a variety of different purposes. It is therefore worth exploring briefly the rationale behind different types of models in order to understand the scope and nature of the model being proposed here. The primary functions of models of learning or e learning that have been developed to date are:

- to support course development (frequently with no reference to business models).
- to support business processes (decision making, control, implementation, funding etc) or
- to support the design of teaching and learning processes.

One of the features that all such models have in common is that they concentrate on only a part of the processes. They neither are conditioned by inputs nor restricted by output This is a major weakness if one is trying to understand the e learning life-cycle since either many of the essential decisions on which aspects of a model depend will already have been taken (explicitly or implicitly) or the implications of a model for dependent processes will not be considered and in either case there is a loss of context for understanding or applying a model.

It is argued that the lack of a complete model or of understanding of where a model fits in a fuller context means that many of the decisions are made implicitly and that this is likely to lead to poorer decision making than could be achieved if a model had been used that makes the decisions explicit.

An examination of three models dealing with different aspects of elearning illustrates these points. A good example of a learning led model is Laurillard's conversational model (Laurillard 2002). The focus of the model is on the student learning, from which she then deduces the characteristics of the design, development and delivery that ensure an effective course. The focus is entirely on the learning and the model itself has little to say about the business models which are needed to ensure the effective delivery of the course around such issues as marketing, recruitment or student support (other than pedagogic support), nor does it have much to say about the processes of design and development that ensure such learning can take place.

The model is developed from the work of Vygotsky (Vygotsky 1962) who proposed that social interaction is fundamental to learning, stating "Every function in the child's cultural development appears twice: first, on the social level, and later, on the individual level; first, between people (interpsychological) and then inside the child (intrapsychological).

This applies equally to voluntary attention, to logical memory, and to the formation of concepts. All the higher functions originate as actual relationships between individuals." (Vygotsky 1978). Laurillard suggests that learning is based on the teacher helping the student to conceptualise the teacher's model of the subject through discussion and negotiation. Laurillard uses this model to propose a design methodology encompassing issues such as designing teaching materials, setting the learning context and even designing an effective organisational infrastructure but these remain high level conceptualisations. In essence, Laurillard's model is one of the teaching and learning process.

A second model type is that of business models, which represents the "architecture for product, service and information flows, including a description of the various business actors and their roles; and a description of the potential benefits for the various business actors; and a description of the sources of revenues" (Timmers 2000). Note that education or teaching and learning are not specified, and that the model type is concerned with business flows rather than any pedagogic issues. A typology of business models that remains at the abstract level is that of Rappa (Rappa 2004), who lists 9 models that deal with the financial 'engine' of an enterprise:

- **Brokerage** - brokers act as intermediaries between buyers and sellers (providers of courses and students), and normally add value either by helping the customer find what they want more easily or negotiate a better deal for them. Brokers usually charge a commission to either the buyer, or the seller or indeed both.
- **Advertising** - This is an extension of the traditional media broadcast model, where the advertising provides the revenue, as with many search engines and free newspapers.
- **Infomediary** - Rappa defines this as data about consumers and their consumption habits are valuable, especially when that information is carefully analysed and used to target marketing campaigns.
- **Merchant** - traditional sales model which may be based on list prices or auctions.
- **Manufacturer (Direct)** - Similar to merchant sales, except that they are direct from the manufacturer
- **Affiliate** - this offers financial incentives (in the form of a percentage of revenue) to affiliated partner sites. The affiliates provide purchase-point click-through to the merchant. It is a pay-for-performance model.
- **Community** - The viability of the community model is based on user loyalty. Users have a high investment in both time and emotion. Revenue can be based on the sale of ancillary products and services or voluntary contributions.
- **Subscription** - Users are charged a fee for using the service on a daily, monthly or annual basis. This is frequently

combined with a free service and a "premium" subscription service.

- **Utility** - this is similar to the subscription model, except that it is pay-per-use rather than per period.

There are other models used in the business aspects of course development such as cost-benefit models. One such that is from the education world is that of the World University Network which has produced a model (WUN 2003) which focuses on the financial issues, stating that "the financial algorithm ... is at the heart of the process." As it goes on to state "few institutions have much experience of the financial aspects of running such courses." Which means that there are few cases where a detailed mapping of business models to e learning have been undertaken. The model looks almost exclusively at the costs involved in developing and delivering e learning, listing:

- Academic development and delivery costs
- Instructional designer costs
- Course Director/Project Manager/Programmer/administrative costs
- Tutor costs
- Other University support staff
- Resource allocation model (This one is an oddity, and the description says "Your institution will have a model for distributing resources amongst its various faculties, departments, university administration, library, computing etc. It will almost certainly be unique to your institution. You need to be careful that it does not include some form of "taxation" which is based on one, all or some of income, student numbers, staff numbers, space utilisation, etc. You should find out what these are at the business planning stage - you don't want any nasty surprises at a later stage!!")
- Computing costs
- Library costs
- Overheads
- Other non-staff costs against expenditure, and
- Student numbers

- It mentions nothing of the financial engine or of other key aspects of business such as vision, strategy and decisions making.
- Module/Programme Fee

A well articulated model dealing with the deeper and development aspects of elearning is that of the UK eUniversities Worldwide (UKeU) (Darby 2001) which defines six approaches to e learning; which look at the focus of development and delivery. They are:

- **e learning in its infancy -** which were "direct analogues of conventionally delivered face-to-face or distance learning courses."
- **Academic sole practitioner -** which Darby argues does not scale to the level needed for something like the UKeU.
- **Support service -** Development is supported through services such as learning technology and staff development which can support staff (or groups of staff) in the development of e learning. This can be seen as a form of staff development, where members of staff are supported in developing their approach to teaching and learning.
- **Course team** - In the UK this is best exemplified by the Open University. The course team prepare a detailed course design, which is approved before production starts, and in the case of the OU a separate production methodology is used for each type of material.
- **Contractor** - There is a separation between the development of courses (by the contractor) and their delivery. Examples include Cardean University with Unext.com.
- **Broker** - UfI is the best known example in the UK, with UfI acting as a broker between course developers, learndirect centres and students.

They then describe an eight stage model for UkeU enterprises of e learning course production based on the OU model that can be seen to fit with the 'Course Team' approach developed by the OU.

1. Identify course opportunity and student demand

2. Select primary academic consultants
3. Prepare course specification
4. Create modules
5. Create linking structure
6. Conduct review
7. Deliver course
8. Maintain and update.

Note again that this model makes no reference to business aspects on the one hand or to actual teaching and learning on the other. Models of business aspects of e-learning or of course development for example have been devised for a variety of reasons. In most cases they are focused on understanding, and so enhancing, some part of the e-learning life-cycle. Few, if any, of the models are designed to support evaluation, hence the need for the new model that we are proposing here, which is specifically designed to support the embedding of effective evaluation within the entire e-learning life-cycle. The point that needs to be emphasises here is a simple yet profound one that, even were such models to encompass evaluation, which most do not, the possibilities for these evaluation processes to work are severely restricted. This is because, dealing only with a part of the life cycle, the dependencies that can be considered or effected are circumscribed. In particular, the dependencies between vision design, development, delivery of teaching and learning and all aspects of renewal that ensure the **coherence** of any life cycle **cannot** exist in such models.

E-Learning is different, in exposing the need to have a life-cycle approach to education provision. In so far as models of development and delivery need to include evaluation in order to be the basis for action, and the argument here is that in any such process, evaluation is **absolutely essential**, then the models presented here are bound to fail.

Types and Functions of Evaluation

With the exception of evaluation as a research tool, the function of evaluation is, in the end, to support the enhancement of quality and to manage risks. However, this does not get us very far unless we can say clearly what we mean by quality; and this depends on the user's quality (what their role is) their objectives and what context.. Unfortunately quality has become a very loaded term in the last few years, with much of the UK sector having a view limited to the scope of the Quality Assurance Agency (QAA). Quality is often defined as "fitness for purpose" and for the present discussion that is an adequate definition. However, even this limited definition takes us well beyond the QAA concept. In order to explore what this means we need to consider types of evaluations and their functions.

Types of Evaluation

There are many reasons for wanting to evaluate, and these are reflected in different types of evaluation that are used.. Oliver (Oliver 2000) describes five types of evaluation:

- **Formative evaluation** - provides information that allows revisions and improvements to be made. Its primary audience usually consists of the project or course team. Formative evaluation is usually carried out by members of the team, it must be timely and in a form that is readily accessible to the team; Oliver argues that in practice this means that utility sometimes takes precedence over validity.
- **Summative (experimental) evaluation** - is concerned with judgement of course outcomes against a standard rather than improvement. Summative evaluations are often carried out by an external evaluator in order to ensure objectivity. However this objectivity is likely to be spurious as any evaluation is undertaken in a cultural professional and political framework which affects the questions asked and the scope of the answers provided. Oliver goes on to argue that this approach has other problems as it is almost impossible to design procedures that are both methodologically sound and also relevant to practice. The difficulty in controlling variables makes it difficult to factor out external influences.
- **Illuminative evaluation** - is an alternative form of Summative evaluation and is concerned with identifying

and exploring the factors in the success of a course that are important to participants.. It is based on ideas from social anthropology and involves the use of observation, inquiry and explanation with a pragmatic approach to analytical methods and the use of triangulation to enhance reliability. It means that the context becomes the focus for the evaluation. It does mean that the results depend on the perceptions of participants and thus cannot be considered *objective.* It does raises particular problems in the case of e learning due to the distributed nature of the student population, which can make observations particularly complex.

- **Integrative evaluation** - this attempts to take elements from Summative and Illuminative evaluation. Oliver writes that "Inherent in the approach is the assumption that the evaluation's findings will be situationally-specific, and as with illuminative evaluation, the results are not generalisable."
- **Evaluation for quality assurance (auditive evaluation) -** This can be used both for ensuring conformance and for identifying good practice; however it can create a climate where negative outcomes are "problematic" and risks may be replaced with compliance leading to performativity. Typically this type of evaluation is external to the course team and is likely to be controlled by a funder or statutory agency.

This typology suggests that we are particularly interested in formative, illuminative and integrative evaluation, rather than summative or auditive evaluation as the focus of the former is more clearly on quality enhancement.

Purposes of Evaluation

So far we have looked at the forms of evaluation; there is a need to look at why we are undertaking the evaluation as well.

Another way of considering evaluation, and probably more usefully here is to look at the purpose of evaluation. Harland (1996) argues that there are three purposes for evaluation (Finch

1986). They are evaluation for action (decision making), evaluation for understanding (enlightenment) and evaluation for control. While it is clear that any evaluation may have elements of all three, what we are concerned with is the emphasis given to each in the evaluation.

Evaluation for Control

A particular purpose for evaluation in the current era of accountability is control. Harland identifies three aspects of this perspective on evaluation: compliance, surveillance and patterning. Compliance consists of judging whether a programme has met pre-defined objectives, processes and outcomes. Surveillance links evaluation with monitoring; it consists of an ongoing process of checking compliance, allowing interventions to be made by management. Patterning is more subtle; it works to influence discourse. It conveys a message to the project team and any audience about the values of the project by requiring the adoption of particular kinds of language. (For example, judging whether a course is 'student-centred' involves the course team re-casting their activities according to whether they are student-centred of not, whether or not they would previously have described them in this way.)

Evaluation for Understanding

This purpose can be described as reflecting an 'enlightenment' approach to evaluation and it has its roots in social research.. The emphasis within this tradition is on conceptual and intellectual development of the evaluator. This is argued to reflect actual as opposed to intended patterns of evaluation use, since "the impact of most (evaluation) is argued to be 'diffuse and indirect' rather than immediate" (Harland, 1996: 92).

Evaluation for Action

This type reflects an 'engineering' approach to evaluation. Its purpose is to provide information that is needed to take particular decisions.

This brings us to Patton's ideas on utilisation-focused evaluation (Patton 1997), which relate to Harland's ideas on evaluation for action. Patton argues that many commissioned evaluation studies are simply never read, and rejects the idea that evaluations can be judged as "good" on the basis of the methodology. Instead, he proposes that evaluations should be considered "good" where they help decision-making or action. Moreover, Patton points out that judgements involved in evaluating the success of a programme rely on particular values. Thus for an evaluation to be credible, it must address the values of particular audiences or stakeholders. Importantly, Patton argues that the funders of the evaluation are not the only audience: the participants in the evaluation are also an audience, as may be other stakeholders. As a result, if the evaluation is to be credible to all these groups, they need to share - or at least appreciate - each others' values. For this reason, a vital part of Patton's utilization-focused approach to evaluation involves dialogue between stakeholders so that they can come to understand and respect each others' positions.

Evaluations can be undertaken for control, understanding or action with one of the other two as a subsidiary function. It is proposed that any model arising from this review should be focused upon action; the issue then remaining is whether it also prioritises understanding or control.

Quality Assurance systems have traditionally been associated with control functions, which encourage short-term conformance to standards but which are not helpful in the long term as people rapidly learn how to meet QA requirements without necessarily improving practice. Oppenheimer (Oppenheimer 2003) talking about standardised examinations comments that "each test reigned for about five years, before being replaced by a new, improved version" as people learn to pass the test rather than learn, and much the same sort of effect is suspected in QA of HE courses. Evaluation for understanding requires greater faith in the professionalism of practitioners but promises long-term quality gains through ongoing reflection and a developed understanding of practice. Evaluation can be carried out by practitioners or by external evaluators, and may consist solely of individual reflection or involve empirical data; those that involve multiple perspectives/ value systems and gathered data tend to be more credible.

However, as we have already noted, a "good" evaluation is of little use unless it is acted on.

With a primary objective of evaluation being action there are a number of commonly adopted options in techniques used for evaluation depending on the secondary objective i.e. understanding or control. Which is chosen will reflect the particular needs of the organisation and the stage of the process that is being considered as well as who the evaluation is for (internal to the project, external to the project and internal to the organisation or for an external organisation).

The idea that evaluation for action can be combined with either understanding or control; and that the techniques associated with each of these are different, with those associated with control being more prescriptive, and those for understanding more open-ended.

Underlying this review is a concern with evaluation as a tool for quality enhancement, and thus we are less concerned with type of evaluation (formative, illuminative, integrative, summative and auditive evaluation) than its purpose (action, control and understanding). The primary focus is evaluation for action. However, as noted, some techniques are better suited than others to evaluation for action for reasons of timeliness (the evaluation must be undertaken sufficiently early for it to be possible to act on the conclusions), stakeholder buy in (evaluation which includes the stakeholders in its design and execution is more likely to be listened to and acted on) and the information sought.

Stakeholders

It is worth briefly considering who the stakeholders in the e learning life cycle are since this has an important role in determining the function for the evaluation and thus the type of evaluation to be undertaken. These may not be the same as the stakeholders in the evaluation, who will typically form a subset of the stakeholders.

The key stakeholders are:

- **Institution** which will be offering the course and has ultimate legal responsibility for it. As such the institution is likely to focus on evaluation for control as it needs to assure itself that the course meets the institution's rules.

- **Department/faculty/school** who own the course, many of the QA processes and probably the ultimate success of the course.
- **Course team** this includes not just the lecturing staff but also learning technologists, curriculum designers, IT staff, library or information services staff and all the other support staff who are necessary for creating and running a successful e learning course, including:
- Designers,
- Builders, and
- Tutors
- **students**
- **External authorities** - there are many others who are external to the institution such as legal bodies, professional bodies, employers and the government. Few of these are concerned with evaluation for understanding though some will have an interest in auditive or summative evaluation - where the focus is on control.

The different types of stakeholder will have different views of the evaluation and its purpose. The institution or department will have concerns that are both developmental and controlling. They need to know that the course is proceeding satisfactorily, and will also want to support its enhancement and development. While the course team will have some interest in evaluation for control their prime focus will be evaluation for action and understanding. Students may have little interest in any formal evaluation at all (as they are often more concerned with their personal results than evaluation of courses *per se)*, and external authorities are primarily concerned with auditive evaluation so that they can be (re)-assured that the course is proceeding correctly.

We can thus see that since the different stakeholders are looking for different types of information and action from evaluation, there can often be a tension between these, especially between the managerial need for control and audit and course team need for understanding and quality enhancement, even when the membership of these groups overlaps. The proposed model can include all the needs of all these stakeholders and by making the locus and function of the evaluation explicit it can help resolve these conflicts.

The Proposed Model

Before looking at existing situation it is worth briefly outlining the proposed model of the e learning life-cycle. Having outlined the key features of the model the paper will then look at other models of the e learning life-cycle before returning to a detailed exposition of the model and the way in which it can be used to support evaluation for quality enhancement. When starting to develop a new course the first activity should be to look at the reviews and evaluations of previous courses that are similar in order to inform the planning stage. Careful consideration of demand for any such course and issues of other current suppliers and potential supply opportunities within an institution's actual 'resource envelope' have to be addressed. After Planning there is course design and then development followed by teaching and learning (which are really parallel activities) and then return to review. The cycle will then be repeated throughout the life of the course. The planning stage is in many ways the critical one since it is here that it is decided whether or not to develop the course and subsequent iterations of the cycle whether to continue the course, change it or drop it.

The model also describes the main drivers and controls and activities for each phase: Model of e-learning life-cycle below. Drivers and controls are external to the course, in the sense that those involved with developing and delivering the course will have little control over them. They can be both internal to the institution (Institutional course procedures, institutional QA, strategic plan) and external (professional accreditation, external examiners, QAA and legal requirements). Processes are those activities which are needed to develop and deliver the course.

Process Model

We have looked at the various types of evaluation and the way in which different stakeholders are interested in different types of evaluation that meet their particular needs. This chapter is particularly concerned with how evaluation can be used to support quality enhancement, and so the model of e learning has been developed with this function in mind. In order to support evaluation we need a process model, by which we mean a model that focuses on the processes that are involved in the creation and delivery of e-learning, rather than focusing on people, activities or roles.

There is a need for an explicit model of the full e learning life-cycle, since without this it is not possible to determine the most effective points at which to evaluate, nor what those evaluations should be aiming to achieve. Most evaluations cover only a small part of the life-cycle, and there has been little theoretical justification given for the points selected. Indeed, the vast majority have focused on whether e learning is as effective (or more or less effective) as traditional learning and in this context these can be considered largely as irrelevant.

We therefore need to develop a model which allows us to identify the critical points for evaluation as a basis for action together with the stakeholders (or their surrogates) that need to be involved and the decision making that will take place.

LEARNER ACCESS TO TECHNOLOGY

A policy concern at all levels within higher education centers on the extent to which learners are effectively capitalizing on e-learning opportunities. The following broad areas in which opportunities could be enhanced (or, conversely, in which barriers could be removed) could be used in learner surveys and special studies. (Some of these specific subcategories will likely change as technology changes.)

- Access to technology
  - Access to computers
  - Access to the Internet
  - Access to interactive audio-video sites
  - Reducing the costs associated with technology
- Readiness to use technology

  - Better understanding of technology
  - Raising interest in using technology
  - Better training in the use of technology
  - Removing apprehensions regarding the use of technology
- Effectiveness of technology in the learning process
  - Reducing concerns about the impersonal characteristics of technology
  - Removing concerns about the quality of instruction delivered using technology

E-LEARNING AND ELECTRONIC MEDIA

E-learning refers to the use of electronic media and information and communication technologies (ICT) in education. E-learning is broadly inclusive of all forms of educational technology in learning and teaching. E-learning is inclusive of, and is broadly synonymous with multimedia learning, technology-enhanced learning (TEL), computer-based instruction (CBI), computer-based training (CBT), computer-assisted instruction or computer-aided instruction (CAI), internet-based training (IBT), web-based training (WBT), online education, virtual education, virtual learning environments (VLE) (which are also called learning platforms), m-learning, and digital educational collaboration.

These alternative names emphasize a particular aspect, component or delivery method.

E-learning includes numerous types of media that deliver text, audio, images, animation, and streaming video, and includes technology applications and processes such as audio or video tape, satellite TV, CD-ROM, and computer-based learning, as well as local intranet/extranet and web-based learning.

Information and communication systems, whether free-standing or based on either local networks or the Internet in networked learning, underly many e-learning processes.

E-learning can occur in or out of the classroom. It can be self-paced, asynchronous learning or may be instructor-led, synchronous learning. E-learning is suited to distance learning and flexible learning, but it can also be used in conjunction with face-to-face teaching, in which case the term blended learning is commonly used.

It is commonly thought that new technologies make a big difference in education. Many proponents of e-learning believe that everyone must be equipped with basic knowledge of technology, as well as use it as a vehicle for reaching educational goals.

Overview

E-learning refers to the use of technology in learning and education. There are several aspects to describing the intellectual and technical development of e-learning, which can be categorized into discrete areas. These are addressed in turn in the sections of this chapter:

1. e-learning as an educational approach or tool that supports traditional subjects;
2. e-learning as a technological medium that assists in the communication of knowledge, and its development and exchange;
3. e-learning itself as an educational subject; such courses may be called "Computer Studies" or "Information and Communication Technology (ICT)";
4. e-learning administrative tools such as education management information systems (EMIS).

Educational Approach

The extent to which e-learning assists or replaces other learning and teaching approaches is variable, ranging on a continuum from none to fully online distance learning. A variety of descriptive terms have been employed (somewhat inconsistently) to categorize the extent to which technology is used. For example, 'hybrid learning' or 'blended learning' may refer to classroom aids and laptops, or may refer to approaches in which traditional classroom time is reduced but not eliminated, and is replaced with some online learning. 'Distributed learning' may describe either the e-learning component of a hybrid approach, or fully online distance learning environments. Another scheme described the level of technological support as 'web enhanced', 'web supplemented' and 'web dependent'.

Synchronous and Asynchronous

E-learning may either be synchronous or asynchronous. Synchronous learning occurs in real-time, with all participants interacting at the same time, while asynchronous learning is self-paced and allows participants to engage in the exchange of ideas or information without the dependency of other participants involvement at the same time.

Synchronous learning involves the exchange of ideas and information with one or more participants during the same period of time. A face-to-face discussion is an example of synchronous communications. In e-learning environments, examples of synchronous communications include online real-time live teacher instruction and feedback, Skype conversations, or chat rooms or virtual classrooms where everyone is online and working collaboratively at the same time.

Asynchronous learning may use technologies such as email, blogs, wikis, and discussion boards, as well as web-supported textbooks, hypertext documents, audio video courses, and social networking using web 2.0. At the professional educational level, training may include virtual operating rooms. Asynchronous learning is particularly beneficial for students who have health problems or have child care responsibilities and regularly leaving the home to attend lectures is difficult. They have the opportunity to complete their work in a low stress environment and within a more flexible timeframe. In *asynchronous* online courses, students proceed at their own pace. If they need to listen to a lecture a second time, or think about a question for awhile, they may do so without fearing that they will hold back the rest of the class. Through online courses, students can earn their diplomas more quickly, or repeat failed courses without the embarrassment of being in a class with younger students. Students also have access to an incredible variety of enrichment courses in online learning, and can participate in college courses, internships, sports, or work and still graduate with their class. Both the asynchronous and synchronous methods rely heavily on self-motivation, self-discipline, and the ability to communicate in writing effectively.

Linear Learning

Computer-based learning or training (CBT) refers to self-paced learning activities delivered on a computer or handheld device such as a tablet or smartphone. CBT often delivers content via CD-ROM, and typically presents content in a linear fashion, much like reading an online book or manual. For this reason, CBT is often used to teach static processes, such as using software or completing mathematical equations. Computer-based training is conceptually similar to web-based training (WBT), the primary difference being that WBTs are delivered via Internet using a web browser.

Assessing learning in a CBT is often by assessments that can be easily scored by a computer such as multiple choice questions, drag-and-drop, radio button, simulation or other interactive means. Assessments are easily scored and recorded via online software, providing immediate end-user feedback and completion status. Users are often able to print completion records in the form of certificates.

CBTs provide learning stimulus beyond traditional learning methodology from textbook, manual, or classroom-based instruction. For example, CBTs offer user-friendly solutions for satisfying continuing education requirements. Instead of limiting students to attending courses or reading printed manuals, students are able to acquire knowledge and skills through methods that are much more conducive to individual learning preferences. For example, CBTs offer visual learning benefits through animation or video, not typically offered by any other means.

CBTs can be a good alternative to printed learning materials since rich media, including videos or animations, can easily be embedded to enhance the learning.

However, CBTs pose some learning challenges. Typically the creation of effective CBTs requires enormous resources. The software for developing CBTs (such as Flash orAdobe Director) is often more complex than a subject matter expert or teacher is able to use. In addition, the lack of human interaction can limit both the type of content that can be presented as well as the type of assessment that can be performed. Many learning organizations are beginning to use smaller CBT/WBT activities as part of a broader online learning program which may include online discussion or other interactive elements.

Collaborative Learning

Computer-supported collaborative learning (CSCL) uses instructional methods designed to encourage or require students to work together on learning tasks. CSCL is similar in concept to the terminology, "e-learning 2.0".

Collaborative learning is distinguishable from the traditional approach to instruction in which the instructor is the principal source of knowledge and skills.

For example, the neologism "e-learning 1.0" refers to the direct transfer method in computer-based learning and training systems (CBL). In contrast to the linear delivery of content, often directly from the instructor's material, CSCL uses blogs, wikis, and cloud-based document portals (such as Google Docs and Dropbox).

With technological Web 2.0 advances, sharing information between multiple people in a network has become much easier and use has increased. One of the main reasons for its usage states that it is "a breeding ground for creative and engaging educational endeavours."

Using Web 2.0 social tools in the classroom allows for students and teachers to work collaboratively, discuss ideas, and promote information. According to Sendall (2008), blogs, wikis, and social networking skills are found to be significantly useful in the classroom. After initial instruction on using the tools, students also reported an increase in knowledge and comfort level for using Web 2.0 tools. The collaborative tools also prepare students with technology skills necessary in today's workforce.

Locus of control remains an important consideration in successful engagement of e-learners. According to the work of Cassandra B. Whyte, the continuing attention to aspects of motivation and success in regard to e-learning should be kept in context and concert with other educational efforts. Information about motivational tendencies can help educators, psychologists, and technologists develop insights to help students perform better academically.

Classroom 2.0

Classroom 2.0 refers to online multi-user virtual environments (MUVEs) that connect schools across geographical frontiers. Also known as "eTwinning", computer-supported collaborative learning (CSCL) allows learners in one school to communicate with learners in another that they would not get to know otherwise, enhancing educational outcomes and cultural integration. Examples of classroom 2.0 applications are Blogger and Skype.

E-learning 2.0

E-learning 2.0 is a type of computer-supported collaborative learning (CSCL) system that developed with the emergence of Web 2.0. From an e-learning 2.0 perspective, conventional e-learning systems were based on instructional packets, which were delivered to students using assignments. Assignments were evaluated by the teacher. In contrast, the new e-learning places increased emphasis on social learning and use of social software such as blogs, wikis, podcasts and virtual worlds such as *Second Life*. E-learning 2.0, in contrast to e-learning systems not based on CSCL, assumes that knowledge (as meaning and understanding) is socially constructed. Learning takes place through conversations about content and grounded interaction about problems and actions. Advocates of social learning claim that one of the best ways to learn something is to teach it to others.

In addition to virtual classroom environments, social networks have become an important part of E-learning 2.0. Social networks have been used to foster online learning communities around subjects as diverse as test preparation and language education. Mobile Assisted Language Learning (MALL) is the use of handheld computers or cell phones to assist in language learning. Traditional educators may not promote social networking unless they are communicating with their own colleagues.

Technology

Various technologies are used to facilitate e-learning. Most e-learning uses combinations of these techniques, including blogs, collaborative software, ePortfolios, and virtual classrooms.

Audio

The radio has been around for a long time and has been used in educational classrooms. Recent technologies have allowed classroom teachers to stream audio over the internet. There are also webcasts and podcasts available over the internet for students and teachers to download. For example, iTunes has various podcasts available on a variety of subjects that can be downloaded for free.

Video

Videos allow teachers to reach students who are visual learners and tend to learn best by seeing the material rather than hearing or reading about it. Teachers can access video clips through the internet instead of relying on DVDs or VHS tapes. Websites like YouTube are used by many teachers. Teachers can use messaging programs such as Skype, Adobe Connect, or webcams, to interact with guest speakers and other experts. Interactive video games are being integrated in the curriculum at both K-12 and higher education institutions. Research on the use of video in lessons is preliminary, but early results show an increased retention and better results when video is used in a lesson. Creating a systematic video development method holds promise for creating video models that positively impact student learning.

Computers, Tablets and Mobile Devices

Computers and tablets allow students and teachers access to websites and other programs, such as Microsoft Word, PowerPoint, PDF files, and images. Many mobile devices support m-learning.

Blogging

Blogs allow students and teachers to post their thoughts, ideas, and comments on a website. Blogging allows students and instructors to share their thoughts and comments on the thoughts of others which could create an interactive learning environment.

Webcams

The development of webcams and webcasting has facilitated the creation of virtual classrooms and virtual learning environments.

Virtual classrooms supported by such technology are becoming more and more popular, especially since they are contributing as a main solution to solving problems with travel expenses. Virtual classrooms with such technology also provide the benefits of being easy to set up.

Whiteboards

Interactive whiteboards ("smartboards") allow teachers and students to write on the touch screen, so learning becomes interactive and engaging.

Screencasting

Screencasting is a recent trend in e-learning. There are many screencasting tools available that allow users to share their screens directly from their browser and make the video available online so that the viewers can stream the video directly. The advantage of such tools is that it gives the presenter the ability to show his ideas and flow of thoughts rather than simply explain them, which may be more confusing when delivered via simple text instructions.

With the combination of video and audio, the expert can mimic the one-on-one experience of the classroom and deliver clear, complete instructions. From the learner's point of view this provides the ability to pause and rewind and gives the learners the advantage of moving at their own pace, something a classroom cannot always offer.

Combining Technology

Along with the terms *learning technology, instructional technology,* the term educational technology refers to the use of technology in learning in a much broader sense than the computer-based training or *Computer Aided Instruction* of the 1980s. It is also broader than the terms *Online Learning* or *Online Education* which generally refer to purely web-based learning. In cases where mobile technologies are used, the term M-learning has become more common. E-learning, however, also has implications beyond just the technology and refers to the actual learning that takes place using these systems.

In higher education especially, the increasing tendency is to create a virtual learning environment (VLE) (which is sometimes combined with a Management Information System (MIS) to create a Managed Learning Environment) in which all aspects of a course are handled through a consistent user interface standard throughout the institution. A growing number of physical universities, as well as newer online-only colleges, have begun to offer a select set of academic degree and certificate programs via the Internet at a wide range of levels and in a wide range of disciplines. While some programs require students to attend some campus classes or orientations, many are delivered completely online. In addition, several universities offer online student support services, such as online advising and registration, e-counseling, online textbook purchases, student governments and student newspapers.

E-learning can also refer to educational websites such as those offering learning scenarios, worksheets and interactive exercises for children. The term is also used extensively in the business sector where it generally refers to cost-effective online training.

Virtual Classroom

Virtual Learning Environments (VLE), also known as learning platforms, utilize virtual classrooms and meetings which often use a mix of communication technologies. One example of web conferencing software that enables students and instructors to communicate with each other via webcam, microphone, and real-time chatting in a group setting, is Adobe Connect, which is sometimes used for meetings and presentations. Participants in a virtual classroom can also use icons called emoticons to communicate feelings and responses to questions or statements. Students are able to 'write on the board' and even share their desktop, when given rights by the teacher. Other communication technologies available in a virtual classroom include text notes, microphone rights, and breakout sessions. Breakout sessions allow the participants to work collaboratively in a small group setting to accomplish a task as well as allow the teacher to have private conversations with his or her students.

The virtual classroom also provides the opportunity for students to receive direct instruction from a qualified teacher in an interactive environment.

Students have direct and immediate access to their instructor for instant feedback and direction. The virtual classroom also provides a structured schedule of classes, which can be helpful for students who may find the freedom of asynchronous learning to be overwhelming. In addition, the virtual classroom provides a social learning environment that replicates the traditional "brick and mortar" classroom.

Most virtual classroom applications provide a recording feature. Each class is recorded and stored on a server, which allows for instant playback of any class over the course of the school year. This can be extremely useful for students to review material and concepts for an upcoming exam. This also provides students with the opportunity to watch any class that they may have missed, so that they do not fall behind. It also gives parents the ability to monitor any classroom to ensure that they are satisfied with the education their child is receiving.

FUTURE DIRECTIONS FOR E-LEARNING

What we might conclude from the above is that there has been an insufficient level of attention given to the nature of teaching and learning practice in elearning developments to date. This is understandable since there have been major barriers to overcome in the form of implementing the technical infrastructure, professional training and getting staff and students on board with the idea of elearning. We discuss ways in which current developments may help to establish a greater focus on teaching and learning in the future. In particular we focus on the following:

Learning Activities and Learning Design

We have presented above suggests that for pedagogical innovation using elearning tools to become a reality, both software designers and educators alike need to shift their thinking from a focus on course management to include the design of learning activities themselves.

Significant steps have already begun to be taken in this direction in the development world. The first major contribution was the development of EML (educational modelling language) by Rob Koper and his colleagues at the OUNL in the Netherlands. The work involved in the development of EML has more recently fed into the construction of the IMS Learning Design Specification.

The development of EML which began 1998 was spurred by a dissatisfaction with several features of what we have thus far characterised here as the prevailing model of elearning to date; that is a heavy focus on content or learning objects and an inclination towards information transmission as the overriding yet implicit pedagogical model.

The OUNL team, by contrast wanted to provide a language to explicitly model the interactions involved in a given teaching and learning situation so that this could be incorporated into the design of a learning activity. EML was developed as the notational system for modelling 'units of study', which is their abstraction of a learning activity (e.g. a course, a module, a lesson etc).

This is a departure from the prevailing learning objects model of elearning design, which is centred on units of content and metadata rather than units of activity. The major problem with the learning objects model, argue the EML designers, is that it fails to provide a coherent framework that can express semantic relationships between the learning objects in an educational context. EML is designed to provide a way to type objects according to their pedagogical use, derived from a pedagogical meta-model. The rationale behind the construction of the pedagogical meta-model is described in Koper (2001).

The main contribution of EML to the elearning community at large is that it has played a core role in the development of the

IMS learning design specification. The primary aim of the learning design specification is to allow teachers or designers to describe a learning design in a standardised way that means it could be 'run' in a variety of learning-design aware players or environments.

Unfortunately there are currently no environments that can take an existing learning design and run it, also there is a paucity of tools available to assist in creating a learning design. However, there are two recent developments that are worthy of mention here.

The first of these is LAMS (Learning Activity Management System) LAMS is a learning design inspired system for the creation and running of learning designs in the form of sequences of learning activities and is reviewed as part of this report. The second development in the space is the RELOAD project. This project funded under the JISC X4L Program is engaged in producing tools for the creation, editing and running of both learning objects and learning activities that implement the appropriate IMS/SCORM specifications. The project is implementing IMS content packaging, simple sequencing and learning design specifications in a suite of open-source tools including a package editor based on the existing PackageIt, a SCORM player for running SCORM 1.3 content and the Colloquia VLE.

These two tools currently still in development point a new direction away from the primacy of content management in VLEs towards systems that make activity-centred learning design using interoperability standards a reality. There are still a variety of difficult technical issues to overcome in creating learning designs in one system and running them in another. However, the fact that this work is underway and is feeding into the further development of the interoperability specifications is a positive step.

7

Using Multimedia for Open Learning

Learning packages can contain, or refer out to, range of other kinds of material. We explored the use of tapes in a separate set of suggestions, but the present set aims to alert you to the questions you should be asking yourself about *any* medium. This could range from CD-ROMs, the Internet, intranets, interactive videos, and anything which adds sounds, still pictures, moving images, graphics to the experience of learners working through open learning materials.

1. **How does the medium help open learners' motivation?** Ideally, any multimedia component should help open learners to want to learn from them. If there are too many steps to getting going with the multimedia elements, there is the danger that learners can be put off and maybe stopped in their tracks.
2. **Can the medium be used to provide some learning-by-doing? Perhaps** the biggest danger with some multimedia packages is that however sophisticated the media used, open learners may only be spectators rather than players. Where it is not possible to cause learners to interact directly with the materials, it remains possible to get them to make decisions, answer questions, summarize conclusions and to write down these for later reference.

3. **Can the medium be used to give open learners feedback?** The danger is that the information presented using multimedia is often fixed, and cannot then respond to what open learners may be thinking about it, or to the problems or misunderstandings that may be in their minds. It is best to ensure that some self-assessment questions address directly any important information presented in multimedia formats, so that feedback responses can be designed for learners to address such difficulties.
4. **How does the medium help open learners to make sense of things?** There are often excellent answers to this question. For example, sounds pictures, moving images and colourful graphics can all play useful parts in helping open learners to get their heads around things with which they have been grappling.
5. **Why is this medium better than other, cheaper media?** For example, why is a computer-based package better than a print-based one? There are many good answers to this question. The best answers are when the medium chosen does something that just cannot be done by other media, for example, moving pictures showing body language and facial expression, where such dimensions are crucially important for getting particular messages or attitudes across to open learners.
6. **How relevant will the medium-based element be to the overall learning programme?** One of the dangers with media-based learning is that too much 'nice-to-know' material may be involved, and not enough emphasis placed on 'need-to-know' material, and that open learners may not easily be able to distinguish the two categories.
7. **How will the choice of medium affect open learners' opportunities to learn?** For example, will they only be able to study the particular elements concerned when they are sitting at a networked computer terminal or when logged on to the Internet? Will this mean that they have frequently to stop learning until they can gain such access? Will there be alternative coverage of these elements of

learning for any learners who have not got easy access to the medium, and can it be guaranteed that they will not end up disadvantaged?

8. **How easy will it be to edit and change the medium-based elements?** Open learning materials are never 'finished'. There are always adjustments and changes that are indicated from piloting, feedback from learners and from assessments measuring how well learners actually succeeded in their learning. Some media are much easier to edit and change than others. Changing a CD-ROM or videodisk is a much more complex (and more expensive) business than changing a file in a computer-based package.
9. **What *other* media could have been used?** There is rarely just one way to package up a particular element of learning. It is useful to explore at least two or three alternative ways of using media to deliver each element of learning, and then to make an informed decision about *why* a particular medium is chosen.
10. **How will learners revise and consolidate what they have learnt from the medium?** What will they have to take away? Will they be able to make a structured summary of what they learnt while working with the medium, which will bring all the important points back to their minds when looking at it later?

Using the Internet for open learning

In a way, the Internet is open learning. People can use it at times of their own choice, in their own ways, at their own pace and from anywhere that access to it is available to them. That said, this does not mean that it is automatically a vehicle for productive and effective learning. Indeed, it is very easy to become side-tracked by all sorts of fascinating things, and to stray well away from any intended learning outcome. The suggestions which follow are not intended as starting points for setting out to *deliver* open learning through the Internet (this is indeed possible, but could take a whole book to explore properly), but rather to help open learners to *use* the Internet to obtain material to use in connection with their studies, such as in assignments they are preparing. The following suggestions may help you to help your open learners both to enjoy the Internet *and* to learn well from it.

1. **Play with the Internet yourself.** You need to pick up your own experience of how it feels to tap into such a vast and varied database, before you can design ways of delivering it to your open learners with some meaningful learning experiences.
2. **Decide whether you want your open learners to use the Internet or an Intranet.** An Intranet is where a networked set of computers talk to each other while using Internet conventions, but where the content is not open to the rest of the universe. If you are working in an organization which already has such a network, and if your open learners can make use of this network effectively, there will be some purposes that will be better served by the Intranet. You can also have *controlled* access to the Internet via an Intranet, such as by using hot-links to predetermined external sites.
3. **Use the Internet to research something yourself.** You may well, of course, have already done this often, but if not, give it a try before you think of setting your open learners 'search and retrieve' tasks with Internet. Set yourself a fixed time, perhaps half an hour or even less. Choose a topic that you are going to search for, preferably something a little offbeat. See for yourself how best to use the search engines and compare the efficiency of different engines. Find out for yourself how to deal with 4,593 references to your chosen topic, and how to improve your searching strategy to whittle them down to the ten that you want to use!
4. **Don't just use the Internet as a filing cabinet for your teaching resources!** While it is useful in its own way if your open learners can have access to your own notes and teaching-learning resources, this is not really *using* the Internet. Too many materials designed for use in other forms are already cluttering up the Internet. If all you tend

your open learners to do is to download your notes and printed own copies, sending them e-mailed attachments would do the same job much more efficiently.

5. **Think carefully about your intended learning outcomes.** You may indeed wish to use the Internet as a means whereby your open learners address the existing intended outcomes associated with their subject material. However, it is also worth considering whether you may wish to add further learning outcomes to do with the processes of searching, selecting, retrieving and analysing subject material. If so, you may also need to think about whether, and how, these additional learning outcomes may be assessed.
6. **Give your open learners specific things to do using the Internet.** Make these tasks, where it is relevant, involve up-to-the-minute data or news, rather than where the 'answers' are already encapsulated in easily accessible books or learning resources.
7. **Consider giving your open learners menu of tasks and activities.** They will feel more ownership if they have a significant degree of choice in their Internet tasks. Where you have a group of open learners working on the same syllabus, it can be worth letting them choose different tasks, and then communicating their main findings to each other (and to you) using a computer conference or by e-mail.
8. **Let your open learners know that the process is at least as important as the outcome.** The key skills that they can develop using the Internet include designing an effective search and making decisions about the quality and authenticity of the evidence they find. It is worth designing tasks where you already know of at least some of the evidence you expect them to locate, and remaining open to the fact that they will each uncover at least as much again as you already know about.
9. **Consider designing own interactive pages.** You may want to restrict these to an Intranet, at least at first. You can then

use dialogue boxes to cause your open learners to answer questions, enter data, and so on. Putting such pages up for all to see on the Internet may mean that you get a lot of unsolicited replies!

10. **Consider getting your open learners to design and enter some pages.** This may be best done restricted to an Intranet, at least until your learners have picked up sufficient skills to develop pages that are worth putting up for all to see. The act of designing their own Internet material is one of the most productive ways to help your open learners to develop their critical skills at evaluating materials already on the Internet.

OPEN LEARNING

Motivation is typically defined as the force that accounts for the arousal, selection, direction, and continuation of behaviour. Motivation means the desire and willingness to do something. It is a drive that compels an individual to act towards the attainment of some goal. As defined by Daft, "Motivation refers to the forces either within or external to a person that arouse enthusiasm and persistence to pursue a certain course of action." Motivation plays a crucial role in learning. It not only sets in motion the activity resulting in learning, but also sustains and directs it. It is "the central factor in the effective management of the process of learning" (Kelley, 2002, as cited in Aggarwal, 2004). Academic motivation has been found to be positively associated with academic achievement, academic performance, and the "will to learn" (McCelland et al., 1953; Entwistle, 1968; Frymier et al., 1975). Various studies have found that classroom competition (Bolocofsky, 1980), family culture and environment, personal aspiration factors, and study habits positively motivate students to do better.

Open learning has afforded opportunities for education outside the realm of the conventional system by providing flexibility in pursuing courses and taking examinations (Gautam, 1990; Indradevi, 1985). Studies have further stated that the popularity and acceptance of open education systems is on the rise. Freedom from constraint may also be seen as a defining feature of distance learning, for example freedom of content, space, medium, access, and relationship development (Anderson, 2006, as cited in Hartnett et al., 2011). Other than flexibility, job-related goals (Wanieweicz, 1981) and improvement of social status are the main motivation to join the open education system. It has also been revealed that the chances of students successfully completing their open education studies is generally linked to their personal concept, capacity for self-management, and familiarity with technology (Schifter & Monolescu, 2000). Notwithstanding the advantages that distance education offer, retention of students has been a major area of concern in open education. Dropout rates reported by open and distance learning (ODL) institutions are typically higher than those reported by conventional universities (Pierrakeas et al., 2004). Pierrakeas et al. (2004) further report the following:

In Europe, dropout rates in distance education programs typically range from 20 percent to 30 percent or even higher in Northern America (Schlosser & Anderson, 1994). Asian countries have recorded rates as high as 50 percent (Shin & Kim, 1999; Narasimharao, 1999).

Various reasons such as family (related to childbirth, child rearing, marriage, pregnancy, travel problems, death of a family member), personal, or health reasons (Pierrakeas et al., 2004), distance to the study centre, insufficient academic support from study centers, absence of interaction with other students, and insufficient counselling sessions (Fozdar et al., 2006) have been found to contribute to higher dropouts in the open education system. Apart from these explicit factors, poor motivation has been identified as a decisive factor in contributing to the high dropout rates from online courses (Muilenburg & Berge, 2005). Against this backdrop of poor retention rates, the diverse characteristics of distance learners and the importance of motivation in the learning process prompted our study. This study explores whether the level of motivation in OES students compared to TES students is low enough to raise apprehension among distance education administrators. Issues have been raised and explored regarding the motivation of students of TES and OES. Further, motivation has been explored from extrinsic and intrinsic points of view. While intrinsic motivation is important to influence the learning habits of students, particularly in OES, this study also examines the importance of extrinsic motivation in the formation of the overall motivation level of students.

Objectives of this Study

Though it may not seem logical to compare the pupils of the two types of education systems, which differ so widely in their characteristics and functioning, the researchers have undertaken this study to explore the reasons, if any, for the differences in motivation levels.

The study aims to discover the learning motivations of OES and TES students. The study compares academic motivation between the two education systems. It also incorporates a comparison between male and female students studying under the two systems. The various dimensions that have influence on the motivation level of students are discussed.

The objective of this study is also to apply the theories of motivation to explore the reasons for any significant differences in the motivation levels of the two types of pupil. This study will present suggestions which may be beneficial for policy makers. It will also raise questions which may be the subject matter of future research. To achieve the above stated objectives and after reviewing the related literature the following hypotheses have been framed and tested.

Hypothesis 1: There is no significant difference in the academic motivation of students studying in the two systems of education.

Hypothesis 2: There is no significant difference in the academic motivation of male and female students studying in the two systems of education.

Hypothesis 2 has further been subdivided into the following hypotheses.

Hypothesis 2(a): There is no significant difference in the academic motivation of the male and female students studying in the traditional education system.

Hypothesis 2(b): There is no significant difference in the academic motivation of the male and female students studying in the open education system.

Hypothesis 2(c): There is no significant difference in the academic motivation of the male students studying in the traditional education system and in the open education system.

Hypothesis 2(d): There is no significant difference in the academic motivation of the female students studying in the traditional education system and in the open education system.

Delimitations of this Study

The present study has the following delimitations:

- It is confined to undergraduate students only.
- It is confined to two faculties, namely the arts and science faculties.
- The population under study is limited to the municipal limits of Allahabad Municipal Area (Uttar Pradesh, India).
- The sample size of the present study is limited to 351 students.
- The present study is limited in its design, method, measuring devices, and statistical techniques.

Method

The present study is closely connected with the normative survey method of research. The population for the present study has been defined as all B.A. and B.Sc. students (male and female) of session 2009-2010 studying in the degree colleges affiliated to Allahabad University and Allahabad study centre of U.P. Rajarshi Tandon Open University who have gone through the process of examination and evaluation of their respective educational system at least once.

The population for the traditional education system has been defined as the number of students studying in the degree colleges offering B.Sc. and B.A. courses in Allahabad city region; these degree colleges are affiliated to the University of Allahabad. Only second and third year undergraduate students have been considered as members of the population as they have gone through the examination and evaluation process of their education system. At the time of the study, a total population of 13,748 students from nine colleges was eligible to participate.

The population for the open education system has been defined as the number of students enrolled with Uttar Pradesh Rajarshi Tandon Open University, Allahabad, for the courses in the arts and science streams.

Their study centers are based in Allahabad. This university conducts examinations each semester, which is why the population constitutes all the students studying in the first, second, and third years of their respective stream ($n = 305$ from five study centers). Those first year students considered to be part of the population have appeared and cleared their first-semester examination, thus fulfilling the criterion of "going through the examination and evaluation process."

Sample Size

In the present study a stratified random sampling method has been used as Miller pointed out that "the essential requirement of any sample is that it is as representative as possible of the population or the universe from which it has been drawn."

Instruments

The questionnaire used in the present study is primarily a self-developed tool named the Academic Motivation Scale (AMS). A few other standard questionnaires were studied to find their suitability for the present study.

No published tool was found suitable by the authors in its exact original form as none catered to the needs of college going students of TES and OES. Development of this instrument has taken inputs from the one that was published and developed by Srivastava (1974) with the title Academic Motivation Inventory.

This tool is adapted to Indian conditions and is meant to test the academic motivation of secondary school students. There are 58 items in the tool of which 29 items are positive and 29 negative.

This instrument has three dimensions, namely academic aspiration (22 statements), study habits (20 statements) and attitude toward school (16 statements).

The questionnaire used in this study has taken help from the standardized tool developed by Srivastava. The present tool has retained the three dimensions of the Academic Motivation Inventory and added another dimension, social-family-economic (environment).

Since college students, whether under TES or OES, have more exposure and interactions with different elements of society and environment, they are more vulnerable to developing positive or negative academic motivation levels as per their environment. Hence, the dimensions used in the questionnaire are as follows:

- *personal aspiration,*
- *study habits,*
- *social-family-economic (environment) factors,* and
- *attitude towards college/study centre.*

A five-point rating scale was prepared by the researcher with the following alternatives: *strongly agree, agree, undecided, disagree,* and *strongly disagree.*

Having identified the items, the preliminary tool was tested on 40 students consisting of 20 students from TES and 20 students from OES belonging to the science stream or the arts stream. Emphasis was laid upon the inclusion of male, female, rural, and urban students in the proper ratio.

The tool was administered to examine the gross language mistakes and identify the defects, if any. After making the necessary corrections AMS was administered on 150 students.

Final Form of Questionnaire

Nine items due to t-value and five items due to item validity and item difficulty were rejected. Therefore 46 items remained. These 46 items or statements can be deemed as completely fit and appropriate for further use. In the final form of the AMS, there were 15 items for measuring the first dimension (i.e., personal aspiration), 15 items for the second dimension (i.e., study habits), 8 items for the third dimension (i.e., socioeconomic factors), and 8 items for the fourth dimension (i.e., attitude towards college/ study centers).

The final scale (AMS) contained 22 favorable and 24 unfavorable statements. The tool was standardized by judging reliability using the split half method (the correlation coefficient was found to be 0.87 and when corrected it was 0.93) and test-reset method (moment product correlation coefficient was 0.97) and incorporating suggestions from students, educationists, psychologists, and specialists working in the field of education (traditional as well as open).

Brief Description of Dimensions of AMS

The following four dimensions have been taken in designing AMS to analyse the academic motivation of students, keeping in mind the characteristics of the research population.

Personal aspiration

This is an intrinsic motivation that energizes an individual to perform certain tasks. It is the main driving force that guides a student through the process of learning.

A stronger feeling of self-determination and competence will have a positive impact on the development of a student's academic motivation, whereas the opposite will have a negative impact (Deci & Ryan, 1991, cited in Karsenti, 1999).

Study habits

Habit is customary behaviour or something that a person does naturally and enjoys doing. Analysis of an individual's habit pattern reflects the level of commitment and determination regarding certain tasks.

This domain is a visible component of intrinsic motivation in the form of action and behaviour compared to personal aspiration which is generally not visible. Hull's drive theory (1943) cited in Beck says that drive multiplied by habit produces the excitatory potential for a response: Excitatory potential = habit X drive. Thus, intrinsic motivation when combined with extrinsic motivation may result in the development of good habits (actions) to fulfill the drives (internal) by maximizing potential (efforts). So analysis of study habit patterns is helpful in determining the level of motivation of TES and OES students.

Social-family-economic (environment) factors

Personality and individual differences affect the motivation level and behaviour of a person. The personality traits of an individual are often influenced and governed by environmental factors.

The environment provides various cues and important extrinsic motivation factors to initiate action and energize intrinsic motivation. Hartman (2001) cited in Kawachi (2006) says that cognition, affect, metacognition, and environment are four interrelated dimensions associated with learning.

Attitude towards college/study centre

Attitude is a learned tendency or predisposition to respond in a consistently favorable or unfavorable manner to some concept, situation, or object. Beck (2005) says that cognitive inconsistency occurs when an event is perceived to be different from an expectation.

Such inconsistencies may be arousing and may induce attitude change. In the present study, attitude towards college/study centre refers to the opinion or general feeling the students have towards their college/study centre depending upon the consistency or inconsistency of events with their expectations.

Statistical Technique Used

Statements of the AMS were coded and arranged. Then, the t-test (Garrett, 1981, pp. 243-245) statistical technique was used to investigate the different hypotheses.

Descriptive Analysis of Questionnaire

Analysis of the questionnaire revealed that 177 TES students out of 200 cited "fear of loss of image in family and society" as one of the major motivations to study many hours to clear the exam successfully.

But no such fear was found among OES students; instead, these students wanted to successfully complete the course for their satisfaction and for future career advancement. Students of both systems acknowledged the importance of higher education in achieving elevated career and social growth, but, surprisingly, a majority of students from both education systems emphasized that clearing the examination was more important than enhancing their conceptual understanding of the subject matter (76% under TES and 93% under OES).

The majority of OES students (71%) cited various excuses (lack of time, inaccessibility of tutor and peers to solve doubts, problems with course material, etc.) for not being able to study regularly. Similarly, 91% of OES students were dedicated to fulfilling their job and family responsibilities, making learning secondary.

Results and Discussion

Overall, the present study concludes that there is significant difference in the levels of academic motivation between TES and OES students.

The results further show that TES students are more motivated than OES students. On all dimensions, TES students have scored higher means compared to OES students. Students of OES are found to be low on personal aspiration and study habits and less motivated, and they do not have much of a positive attitude towards their study centers.

Differences in the means of the two types of students is greater in the study habits and personal aspiration dimensions. This suggests that regular classroom studies, regular teacher-student interaction, regular discussions among students, availability of library facilities, and so on help develop better study habits in TES students.

Further, it can be concluded that due to the different social environment settings of the students, there are differences in motivation levels. TES students generally are more conscious about their family and society.

Analysis of different statements suggests that parents and society play a major role in the academic decision-making process of these students. They feel it is important and prestigious to attain a good position in their studies.

On the other hand, OES students are self-reliant and are generally engaged in some other occupation. Their first priorities may be job, family, or other things rather than devoting regular time towards studies.

Their personal aspiration extends merely to passing the examination and obtaining the degree. This results in poor study habits. It is the intrinsic motivation which drives the students' will to learn in OES. It is also seen from the descriptive analysis of the questionnaire that a majority of students (in both TES and OES) have a superficial approach to learning habits. The AMS statements used in this research have integrated the factors explained by Kawachi (2006). Analysis of the questionnaire shows that OES learners have lower average scores on these factors compared to TES learners.

It can be concluded that extrinsic motivation is not prominent in OES students. On the other hand, extrinsic motivation is an important factor along with intrinsic motivation in TES students. Beck (2005, p. 257, 264) has stated that anxiety and frustration are strongly motivating.

This study concludes that there are lower amounts of anxiety and frustration in OES students with respect to their learning habits. The reasons for lower frustration and lower anxiety are mainly related to the immediate results that TES and OES produce. TES students see immediately the results of their studies as their degrees make them eligible for various competitive exams and job opportunities.

Thus immediate rewards are associated with effort by the students of TES. On the other hand, for a large section of OES students, no such immediate reward is perceived as most of them are preengaged with other commitments.

The following conclusions can be generalized.

- TES students show better study habits as there are immediate rewards and punishment.
- TES students have more regular study habits mainly due to their regular classroom teaching and peer interactions than OES students.
- The academic environment in TES colleges has a positive motivation on these students compared to OES students.
- Extrinsic motivation has a greater and immediate effect on the motivation level of TES students. Intrinsic motivation is a governing factor in the accomplishments in OES. Since extrinsic motivation is not as valuable for the students of OES, their overall motivation level is low.
- Gender-wise analysis shows that the motivation levels of male and female students of one system compared to the levels of male and female students of the other system differ significantly.

We see that OES students are low in extrinsic motivation, which results in an overall lower motivation level. The difference in the levels of motivation between students of TES and OES is significant.

To increase the extrinsic motivation level, recognition and worth of the degrees obtained from OES should be increased. The importance of extrinsic motivation has also been acknowledged by Hartnett et al. (2011) in their recent research: "While intrinsic motivation constituted an important part of students' motivation to learn in the contexts described here, identified regulation (i.e., recognising the value and importance of the activity) was also important."

Policy makers are gradually increasing the worth of degrees procured under OES by making these degrees eligible for students to appear for job interviews and write various competitive examinations.

This trend is also evident from the fact that, these days, various advertisements published by institutions/universities offering courses through distance learning are highlighting the equivalence of these degrees to the degrees of TES as far as eligibility for competitive examinations.

This can be said to be a step in the right direction but it is also true that such degree holders must be capable to stand at par in knowledge and skills with the students of the traditional education system, which is why the evaluation process of OES becomes important to assure quality.

Facilities at the study centers should be improved and involvement of students in the academic process should be increased under OES to develop positive attitudes towards their education system. The role and intervention of tutors along with peer interaction are of paramount importance in developing motivation among students to learn.

The basic natures of the two systems are different and so require altogether different approaches to run and manage the education process.

The traditional education system depends more on verbal communication and methodologies to impart education thus making it quick and having an immediate effect (in the form of immediate rewards and feedback). On the other hand, the education process of OES is largely completed through written or other media communication involving distances and depends upon many intermediaries.

Consequently, the types of skills required in faculty members, students, and administrative personnel are significantly different in the two types of education systems. Administrators and faculty members of OES should be able to design study materials in a way that is effective and easy to comprehend by the students. The importance of administrative roles increases in OES so that course materials and feedback/evaluation are available to students on time and records are updated continuously and correctly. The role of administrators and tutors can also be stretched to keep track of failing students and to guide them towards successful completion of the course by sending motivating letters.

Research can be undertaken to investigate if there is a positive relationship between the personality traits of students pursuing education through OES and successful course completion. Such traits, if any, can be identified and used to formulate policies and strategies for effective governance of OES.

Registration and entrance tests may contain a few questions or statements designed to help judge the personality traits of prospective candidates seeking admission to OES courses. This may help in formulating strategies and policies to reduce the dropout rates. The time required to complete a syllabus should be known to OES students beforehand to make them aware of the time and energy they need to put in for successful completion of the course.

In summary, enhancing infrastructure facilities, increasing the worth of degrees, increasing the roles of tutors, and increasing familiarity with technology and administrative correctness and innovation are paramount in OES to lessen the motivation differences between the students of the two systems.

USING E-MAIL TO SUPPORT OPEN LEARNING

Electronic communication is addictive! To most people who have already climbed the learning curve of finding out how to use e-mail, the apprehension they may have experienced on their first encounters fades into insignificance. E-mail can be an important medium in open learning. The following suggestions may help you to maximize some of the benefits it can offer to you and to your learners.

1. **Make sure that learners get started with e-mail.** Write careful, step-by-step briefing instructions for you learners. The computer literate people may hardly do more than glance at these before getting into the swing of using e-mail. However, for those people who lack confidence or experience with computers, these instructions can be vital and com-forting until they become familiar with the medium.
2. **Decide what you really want to do with e-mail.** There are numerous purposes that e-mail can serve, and you need to ensure that the purpose is always clear to your learners. If they know *what* it is being used for, and *why* e-mail has

been chosen for this, they are much likely to get more out of it.

3. **Make the most of e-mail.** Although you may just want be use e-mail for routine communication with (and between) learners, there are many more uses that the medium can lend itself to. Think about the possible uses of sending attached files, such as documents, assignments, digitally-stored images, sounds and video recordings. All of these can be edited or marked, and returned to learners, in the same ways as simple messages.
4. **Make most messages really brief and to the point.** Few people take much notice of long e-mail messages. If something takes more than one screen, most readers either dump them or file them. Also encourage your learners to make good use of the medium, and to send several short messages rather than to try cramming lots of points into a single missive.
5. **Take particular care with your e-mail message titles.** It can take ages to search for a particular e-mail if it is not clear what each message is about. The computer software can sort messages by date and by sender, but it is more difficult to track down topics. Two or three well chosen keywords make the most useful titles.
6. **When you send a long e-mail, explain why and what to do with it.** For example, from time to time you may want to send learners something that you do not expect them to treat as a normal e-mail message, but perhaps to print out and study in depth. It makes all the difference if they know what they are expected to do with longer messages.
7. **Think about using e-mail to give feedback on assessed work.** It can be much quicker to compose e-mail replies to individual learners than to annotate their written work. It is also quite easy to give feedback on work submitted electronically, such as by adding *your* comments and notes in upper case to distinguish them from the original work, or (if your system permits this) by using a different colour or an alternative font for your feedback.

8. **Make the most of the lack of time constraints.** One of the most significant advantages of e-mail as a vehicle for feedback is that learners can view the feedback when they have time to make sense of it. They can store it until such time becomes available. They can also look at it as often as they wish to, and you can keep copies of exactly what you said to each individual learner.
9. **Be available!** When learners are accustomed to e-mail, they expect quick replies to their queries. If you are going to be away from your access to the system for more than a day or two at a time, it is worth letting all your learners know when you will be back online.
10. **Make the most of the speed.** Giving feedback by e-mail to learners at a distance obviously reduces delays. The sooner learners get feedback on their work, the more likely it is that their own thinking is still fresh in their minds, and the feedback is therefore better understood.
11. **Encourage learners to reply about your feedback.** This lets you know that it has been received but, more importantly, gives them the chance to let you know how they *feel* about the feedback you have given to them, or the mark or grade that you have awarded them.
12. **Use e-mail to keep a dispersed or distant group of learners together.** Sending out circular notes not only helps individuals to feel part of a community of learners, but also reminds them about important matters such as assessment deadlines, or problems that have arisen with course materials or updates to interesting materials that have been discovered on the Internet.
13. **Remember those learners whose access to e-mail is difficult or impossible.** One of the disadvantages of using e-mail as a means of communication on open learning programmes is, that if some learners have problems with access, they can become .... disadvantaged. You may need to find ways of compensating through other means for those things they miss out on.

Using computer conferencing for open learning

There are several parallel names for this, including computer-mediated communication (CMC), computer-supported cooperative learning and, more simply, online learning.

Whatever we call them, computer conferences can be of great value in open learning schemes, especially where the learners are geographically dispersed, but working on similar timescales. Many of the suggestions made about e-mail continue to apply, but in this section I would like to alert you to some of the additional factors to consider with computer conferences.

The following suggestions may help you to maximize the benefits that your learners can derive from computer conferencing.

1. **Note the differences between computer conferencing and other forms of electronic communication.** The distinguishing feature of computer conferencing is that many people can see the same contents from different places and at any time. The contents 'grow' as further notes and replies are added by participants. Most systems automatically alert participants to 'new messages' that have been added since they last viewed the conference, and allow these messages to be read first if desired.
2. **Regard computer conferences as virtual classrooms, seminar rooms and libraries.** Computer conferences can be each of these. They can provide a virtual classroom, where the whole student group can 'meet'. They can be used to provide a virtual seminar room, closed to all but a small learning group of around six students. They can function as virtual libraries, where resource banks and materials are kept. They can also function as student-only gossip areas. Each of these ways of using computer conferences can emulate electronically the related best practice in face-to-face learning environments.
3. **Get involved in computer conferencing situations yourself first.** If you have access to e-mail or the Internet, one of the best ways to pave the way towards putting

computer conferencing to good use with your open learners is to participate yourself. For example, join some discussion lists and experience at first hand the things that work and the things that go wrong with such means of communication.

4. **Explore the computer conferencing system from which you can choose.** There are several systems available around the world, each with their own formats, features and idiosyncrasies. If most of your open learners are not particularly computer literate, go for a system that makes it as easy as possible to log-on and to add messages.
5. **Make sure that all of your open learners will be able to access all the conferences which you want them to.** Ideally, you may also intend them to be able to download and/ or print chosen extracts from the conference for their own personal study purposes. You can only build a computer conference into an open learning programme as an essential component if all of your learners are able to participate. If the conference is just an optional extra for those able to join it, other learners who cannot may be able to claim to have been disadvantaged.
6. **Provide good 'start-up' pages.** These are essentially the main topics of the conference and are listed sequentially in the main directory of the conference. Conferencing takes place when participants add 'replies' to these pages. The replies are normally listed in the sub-directory of each start-up page in the order in which they are received.
7. **Make each screen speak for itself.** Especially with 'start-up' pages, which introduce each topic in the conference, it is best that the essence of the main message takes up less than a single screen. Further detail can be added in the next few pages (or 'replies'). Encourage learners contributing their own replies to keep them to a single screen whenever possible, and to send several replies with different titles rather than one long reply addressing a number of different aspects.

8. **Use the conference as a notice board.** Get into the habit of making the conference *the* best way to keep up with topical developments in the field of study, as well as administrative matters such as assessment deadlines, guidance for learners preparing assessments, and so on. Try to make it necessary for learners to log-on to the conference regularly; this will result in a greater extent of active contribution by them.
9. **Use the conference as a support mechanism.** This can save a lot of tutor time. Elements of explanation, advice or counselling that otherwise may have had to be sent individually to several different open learners can be put into the conference once only and remain available to all. Whenever your reply to an enquiry or problem raised by an open learner warrants a wider audience, the conference is there to do this.
10. **Make the conference a resource in its own right.** Add some screens of useful resource material, maybe with 'hot-links' to other Internet sources that are relevant. It is useful if some such material is *only* available through the computer conference; this ensures that all your learners will make efforts to use it.
11. **Try to get learners discussing and arguing with each other via the conference.** The best computer conferences are not just tutor-student debates, but are taken over by the students themselves. They can add new topics, and bring a social dimension to the conference.
12. **Consider having some assessed work entered onto the conference.** If learners *have* to make some contributions, they are more likely to ascend the learning curve regarding sending in replies, and to do so more readily in non-assessed elements too. One advantage in having an assessed task 'up on the conference' is that each open learners can see everyone else's attempts, and the standards of work improve very rapidly.
13. **Think about the possibilities afforded by audio-conferencing and video-conferencing.** Either, or both, of

these processes can be used very effectively to support open learners to help them to learn from each other and to reduce their isolation. Some of my suggestions about audiotapes and video, mentioned earlier in this chapter, can be linked with the advice above about interaction and communication, to make audio-conferencing and video-conferencing play valuable roles. In particular, it is important to ensure that there are definite, agreed purposes for each occasion where such conferences are used, as well as the freedom to follow up matters which arise during each conference.

Bibliography

Baumann, P. R.: *Computer assisted instruction programs in geography: five climate programs*, Publications in Geography, Oneonta, New York, 1970.

Bentley, T. : *Learning beyond the Classroom: Education for a Changing World*, London, Routledge. 1998.

Connie L., Rosa Cintrón: *Building a Working Policy for Distance Education*, San Francisco, Jossey-Bass, 1997

Driscoll, M., & Alexander, L.: *Web-Based Training : Using Technology to Design Adult Learning Experiences.* Jossey-Bass Publishers, 2000.

Fishman, Katherine Davis: *The Computer Establishment*, New York: McGraw-Hill, 1981.

Gibson, R. : *Critical Theory and Education*, London, Hodder & Stoughton, 1986.

Goldstine, Herman H.: *The Computer: From Pascal to von Neumann*, Princeton, Princeton University Press, 1972.

Goodlad, John I. : *Educational Renewal: Better Teachers, Better Schools*, San Francisco, Jossey-Bass, 1994.

Grace, G. : *School Leadership: Beyond Educational Management*, London, Falmer, 1995.

Harasim, L.: *Online Education – Perspectives on a New Environment*, New York, NY: Praeger Publishers, 1990.

Harry, Keith: *Higher Education through Open and Distance Learning*, New York: Routledge, 1999.

Horton, W. K.: *Designing Web-Based Training: How to Teach Anyone Anything Anywhere Anytime.* Wiley, 2000.

Hsu, Jeffrey: *A Comprehensive Guide to Computer Bible Study. Up-to-Date Information on the Best Software and Techniques*, Dallas: Word, 1993.

Jeffs, T. and Smith, M. : *Using Informal Education*, Milton Keynes, Open University Press, 1990.

Johnson, Peggy : *Collection Management and Development Institute,* Chicago: American Library Association, 1994.

Kawasaki, Guy: *The Computer Curmudgeon,* Indianapolis: Hayden Books, 1992.

Kennedy, K.J. : *Citizenship Education and the Modern State,* Washington, D.C: Falmer Press, 1997.

Khan B. H.: *Web-based instruction.* Englewood Cliffs: Educational Technology Publications, 2008.

Marcella, R. and Newton, R.: *A New Manual of Classification,* Aldershot, Gower, 1994.

McGivney, V. and Murray, F. : *Adult Education in Development, Methods and Approaches from Changing Societies,* Leicester, NIACE, 1991.

Novotny, Jeanne: *Distance Education in Nursing,* New York, Springer, 2000.

Rastogi, P.N. : *Management of Technology and Innovation : Competing Through Technological Excellence,* Response, Delhi, 2009.

Robert A.: *Computer Assisted Tools for Septuagint Analysis,* 1986.

Rogers, A. : *Adults Learning for Development,* London, Cassell, 1992.

Rosenberg, M.: *E-Learning: Strategies for Delivering Knowledge in the Digital Age.* McGraw-Hill, 2000.

Salmon, Gilly: *E-Moderating: The Key to Teaching and Learning Online.* London: Kogan Page or Sterling, VA: Stylus Publishing, 2000.

Simkins, T. : *Non-formal Education and Development,* Manchester, Manchester University, 1977.

Steeples, Christine, & Jones, Chris: *Networked Learning: Perspectives and Issues.* London: Springer-Verlag, 2002.

Talstra, Eep: *Computer Assisted Analysis of Biblical Texts,* Amsterdam: Free University Press, 1989.

White, K. M., & Weight, B. H.: *The online teaching guide: A handbook of attitudes,strategies, and techniques for the virtual classroom.* Boston: Allyn and Bacon, 2000.

Index

O

P

Q

S

T

W

❑❑❑

www.ingramcontent.com/pod-product-compliance
Ingram Content Group UK Ltd.
Pitfield, Milton Keynes, MK11 3LW, UK
UKHW041840190726
13854UKWH00002B/634